SLAM DUNK TO GLORY

*The Amazing Story of the 1966 NCAA Season
and the Championship Game
that Changed America*

DAVID
"BIG DADDY D"
LATTIN

WHITE STONE BOOKS
LAKELAND, FLORIDA

12 11 10 09 08 07   10 9 8 7 6 5 4 3 2 1

Slam Dunk to Glory
The Amazing Story of the 1966 NCAA Season
and the Championship Game that Changed America
1-59379-117-8

SLAM DUNK TO GLORY

In memory of my loving mother,
Elsie, for her unconditional love
and for teaching me I can
do all things through Christ
who strengthens me.

In dedication to my son, Clifton.

ACKNOWLEDGEMENTS

For their love and support I want to thank Elaine, my son's wife, granddaughter Mia, grandsons Noah and Chance, granddaughter Oni, grandson Khadeem; also my daughter Leslie, and grand-daughters Natasha, April, and Breeia.

Thanks also to attorney Bobbi Blackwell for her input and tireless energy; many thanks to Tonette Mitchell for her kindness, sacrifices, and endless late hours.

Special thanks to Republic Beverage, the Goldring family, the Block family, and my colleagues.

Last, but not least, thanks to everyone who supported me along the way. To name a few, thanks to J.D. Patterson, Greg Pappas, Chris Pappas, Harris Pappas, attorney Jerry Bonney, Charles Bush, Gary "Cass" Casatelli, Terry Mitchell, Joey Shassie, John Brock, Milton Smartt, Chris Nickolas, Steve Sims, Peter White, Brad Miller, Paul Janho, Frank Santo, Brock Wilson, George Hope, Clarence Franklin, Michael Pollack, Dean Lyons, Chris Riegler, Mick Newsome, George Thomas, Harold Dutton, Graden Taylor, Dr. Nolon Jones, Steve Saxenian, Rick Haas, Lynn Turner, Tim Hudson, Thai Tran, Mr. Mickey and his son Lenny, Paul Miller, Little James, Richard Jones, Wilbert Bass, Val D. Adams, Phil Harris, Elvert Gill, A.B. Butler, and Rock and Roll Denny.

Finally, my thanks to Ron Watkins for his assistance in turning my story into a book.

FOREWORD
BY CLYDE DREXLER

In all great victories, you have to believe to achieve and then give all that you've got to win it. This determination is the heart and soul of The American Dream.

Texas has embraced The American Dream since the first Texans began to settle in wide open spaces, and The Lone Star State has had its share of American legends, from old school Texas Western's awesome David "Big Daddy" Lattin to new school superstar quarterback Vince Young.

I have my rightful place in Texan, and American, history. I broke basketball records and left my mark playing for Sterling High School in Houston, the University of Houston, the Portland Trail Blazers, and in the Olympics, as well as winning an NBA Championship as a Rocket with former University of Houston Phi Slamma Jamma teammate Hakeem Olajuwon.

"Big Daddy" refers to me as the "Best Two Guard" in basketball history. I refer to him as the "Architect of the Slam Dunk," whose legendary shot has thrilled and dazzled thousands of basketball fans throughout the country.

I watched the movie *Glory Road* and was humbled by the sacrifices these young African-American men made to just play basketball; how their drive, heart, and unstoppable spirit allowed them to reach the pinnacle of college basketball—the national title.

This was no small feat in 1966, when America was permeated with racial discrimination and inequality in almost every arena, from education to employment. The fact was that not every American during this time had a shot at achieving their dream. Then, a basketball game changed a nation.

This milestone championship game was played by an all-black unit from Texas Western, led by the determined, skilled, and very intimidating center "Daddy Lattin." In the first seconds of the game, Lattin was able to showcase his signature in-your-face dunk, which set the tone of the game and helped lead to one of the greatest victories and upsets in college sports, both on and off the court.

Lattin scored sixteen points, pulled down nine rebounds, and blocked six shots while sitting out almost eleven minutes due to foul trouble, against the number one ranked college team in the country, the all-white Kentucky Wildcats.

Even more important than Lattin's statistics in this game was that an all-black unit won this championship for the first time in NCAA history and helped to change the racial makeup of college admissions in America.

Under the visionary leadership of Texas Western's color-blind coach, Don Haskins, America saw that it was time to change its discriminatory practices that had wrongfully denied many blacks athletic scholarships.

After this game, the walls started tumbling down, and thousands of deserving minority students, not just athletes, were admitted to colleges all over America. Pat Riley called this landmark game "The Emancipation Proclamation of college basketball."

Lattin, who was the first Texas basketball and college All-American to win both a state high school and national college championship, is not only the king of slam dunks but also a basketball icon. His life is proof that the sky is the limit for those who refuse to give up and keep their feet on solid ground.

Slam Dunk to Glory is a book of guts and glory that shows the unconquerable spirit of a young black boy who became a man and refused to give anything less than his best on his road to glory.

To God be the Glory....We believed!

Texas Proud,

CLYDE "THE GLIDE" DREXLER
(Basketball Legend and Icon, Perennial NBA All-Star, Portland Trailblazer Giant & Trail Blazer Superstar, Rocket NBA Champion, Olympic Gold Champion, Basketball Hall-of-Famer)

CONTENTS

INTRODUCTION

In the middle of a crisp, clear afternoon in Washington D.C., we were ushered into the White House and taken directly to the Oval Office.

It was December 6, 1974, and I was with the Harlem Globetrotters. We were performing at an arena in nearby Baltimore and had been told the team was to be given an award for national service.

We were greeted by President Gerald Ford and the First Lady, Betty. Meadowlark Lemon and Curly Neal were the stars of the team, and Meadowlark was team coach and designated spokesman. The White House photographer there was snapping photographs of us, the bright flashes of the camera capturing each scene in brilliant light. President Ford signed the proclamation that we received later, and then he passed down the line with his wife to greet each of us individually.

When he reached me, he stopped and said, "David Lattin. I remember you. I saw that game in 1966 and enjoyed it very much. It was amazing and made me very proud to be an American. I'm really pleased to have this chance to meet you." He stood chatting for a long minute, then was nudged and moved on.

I was stunned. I was not the star of the Globetrotters. I was one of the "straight men"—the players who actually scored the points and got rebounds—not one of the showmen and stars the audience came to see. I was the last player on the Harlem Globetrotters whose name the president should have known.

But he had not acknowledged me for my play with this team. No, he remembered me from an earlier team, from a single game in which I had played—from my moment in history.

We left after 20 minutes or so, but I was still in awe. I had come a long, long way from the streets of Houston, Texas.

●

Bobby Joe Hill, the other great star of the 1966 championship Texas Western Basketball Team, and I often talked about writing a book about that season. When he died unexpectedly a few years ago, I put the idea aside until I was approached to play a bit part in the motion picture *Glory Road.* I knew that the movie, and the companion book by Coach Don Haskins, would draw enormous attention to the game and surrounding events. It is a compelling story. I should know; I was part of it.

Bobby Joe Hill was no longer there to take part, but I could still write about what it was like for us, for those athletes who actually played the games that season. No one but the black players on the team knew what it was like for us as we entered the all-white Cole Stadium for the championship game; how we felt looking at the all-white referee crew, white reporters, white scorer's table, white cheerleaders, and nearly all white fans. Bobby Joe's brother and a small but very spirited group from his hometown of Highland Park, Michigan, were there to cheer us on.

Winning the NCAA championship that year was the crowning achievement for Coach Haskins, but the victory did not mean to him what it came to mean to us. It could not possibly, since he did not walk in our shoes or come from our neighborhoods. As good a man as he is, and as great a coach as he was, he did not suffer the constant reminders of the inequalities in America that we faced on a daily basis in our schools, public accommodations, and in almost every facet of our lives.

So here is my story as I lived it. I have drawn on a number of sources that have told this unique story from different perspectives. Among them is *And the Walls Came Tumbling Down: Kentucky, Texas Western and the Game that Changed American Sports* by sportswriter Frank Fitzpatrick, *Haskins: The Bear Facts* as told to Ray Sanchez, and many articles and other news coverage of the subject. I am grateful to all of the writers and authors.

Over the years, I have made a point to talk with the other players on that championship team, to understand what the game has meant to them. I thank all of them for their cooperation and feel a tremendous loss not to share this story in the flesh with my good friend Bobby Joe.

Finally, let me say this: Texas Western was not an all-black basketball team. We had several fine white players and one Hispanic, and without them we would never have made it to the NCAA championship game. None of them played that night, for reasons I will write about later. As part of our team, in a perfect world without overt racism, they would have played.

But ours was not a perfect world then, as it is not now. There were reasons why seven black players played that game against an all-white team, reasons deeply rooted in our history and in the times in which we played.

I am proud to have been a small part of bringing about positive change. This is my contribution to history.

CHAPTER 1

YOUR DATE WITH DESTINY

*Destiny itself is like a wonderful wide
tapestry in which every thread is guided
by an unspeakably tender hand, placed
beside another thread and held and
carried by a hundred others.*

RAINER MARIA RILKE
Austro-German Lyric Poet

A LOT OF PEOPLE are talking about dreams these days. It would seem that all we have to do is wish for something and if we wish hard enough, it can be ours. You've probably seen the casualties—enthusiastic but talentless contestants auditioning for a position of celebrity. After an off-tune performance, they look into the camera with pleading eyes. "I know I'll win because this is my dream." When reality kicks in, they are devastated. Unfortunately, dreams are *not* just wishes our hearts make. To be realized, they must be the outcome of an inner light, the expression of God-given talent, and linked to the destiny God has set in place for us. Most times, *it* finds *us* as we are going about the business of life, doing what we were created to do.

Abraham Lincoln, for example, could not have known he would one day become one of America's best-loved presidents, nor could he have anticipated the part he would play in freeing millions of people from slavery. Though it's difficult to believe, the man who crafted the Emancipation Proclamation and delivered the Gettysburg Address was plagued with depression and self doubt. Still, the man whose presidency spanned the horrors of the Civil War pushed forward to fulfill his destiny.

Peter, the impetuous disciple of Jesus, was a simple fisherman, spending his days, and sometimes nights, earning a meager living, doing what he knew to do. No doubt there were many fishermen who worked along the Sea of Galilee, but Jesus saw something special in Peter. He saw a man capable of recognizing and responding to his destiny, someone with the ability to look beyond the obstacles, the limitations, the impossible, someone looking for his destiny. Peter could not have imagined that one day he would be featured in the pages of the Bible, that Jesus would call him a "rock on which he would build his church." He was simply taking care of business with one eye open for opportunities that might come his way.

The great track star Jesse Owens was born in Alabama, the seventh of eleven children. His father was a sharecropper and his grandfather a slave. When he was nine, his family moved to Cleveland, Ohio. When he tried to tell the teacher at his new school that his name was J.C., he was misunderstood. His heavy southern drawl caused the teacher to think he had said Jesse. And yet "Jesse" took advantage of every opportunity. Realizing that he had athletic ability, he worked hard to develop it. In 1936, Jesse's destiny led him to Berlin to compete for the United States in the Summer Olympic Games. Adolf Hitler was using the games to show the world a resurgent Nazi Germany. Much propaganda had gone out promoting the concepts of "Aryan racial superiority" and depicting Africans as inferior beings. In the course of the next week, Jesse Owens won four gold medals, infuriating the Führer and undermining the Third Reich's flimsy canvas of racial hatred and world domination.

Helen Keller was born deaf and blind in a small, rural town in northwest Alabama. And yet she overcame both the darkness and the silence in pursuit of her destiny. Along the way, she became a scholar, an author, a philosopher, and a lecturer. In 1964, Helen was awarded the Presidential Medal of Freedom, the nation's highest civilian award, by President Lyndon B. Johnson. A year later, she was elected to the Women's Hall of Fame at the New York World's Fair. She once told a blind child, "Never bend your head. Always hold it high. Look the world straight in the face." That was the philosophy that took her from formidable personal handicaps to greatness.

David Lattin, Bobby Joe Hill, and the other members of the 1966 Texas Western Basketball Team, like President Lincoln, the Apostle Peter, Jesse Owens, and millions of others were just pursuing the opportunities that came their way. Many schools touted all-white teams, but Texas Western opened its doors. The ability to seize opportunities where they could be found rather than embracing bitterness and resentment put David and his teammates on track with their destinies.

The members of the Texas Western basketball team were simply taking care of business on the night they won a national championship that would literally change their lives and the face of sports forever. It's true that on that magical night as they walked out onto the court, they might have felt the excitement in the air. They might have said to themselves, "There's something special about this night, this game, this particular place and time." They may have even understood the historical nature of the game in which they were about to take part. But one thing is certain, they played the game like they had played every game of the season—with passion.

The rest is history.

•

When Jesus, God's only Son, arrived in the world, a choir of angels sang and a star led worshippers to His birthplace. Most of us, though, arrive without fanfare, future unknown to us, but known to God. Jeremiah 29:11 says, "I know the plans I have for you," declares the LORD, "plans to prosper you and not to harm you, plans to give you hope and a future." Because your destiny is born of God and His doing, it outshines any challenging circumstance, the most impoverished background, the most debilitating handicap. It is not impeded by obstacles or rendered useless by flaws or shortcomings. Your destiny waits for you at the center of God's will.

As you read this incredible story, where the destinies of some special young men came together to make history and change the world as we know it, give heed to the fact that God also has a destiny for you. As David Lattin can tell you, it's likely to explode on the scene when you least expect it and carry you to places you never imagined you would go. Just when you are busy taking care of business, following the path before you, you run straight into your destiny.

GOD ALSO HAS A DESTINY FOR YOU.

•

Your destiny may not include Olympic medals or national championships, but it will ensure your place in the scheme of things. Open your heart. Open your mind. The possibilities are endless. Your destiny awaits you!

CHAPTER 2

HOUSTON

*Only years later, can you really take a look
at it, and say you know maybe they
were playing for something…a lot
more significant. And if they were,
then the right team won.*

KENTUCKY'S PAT RILEY
3 Time NBA Coach of the Year
5 Time Winningest Coach of the Year

THERE WAS A TIME, in the memory of many people still alive, when America was two nations: one black, the other white.

The divide could be seen almost everywhere: in schools, housing, employment, water fountains, municipal swimming pools, on buses, in the all-white newsrooms of major newspapers, in the face of corporate America, and in the white faces of our nation's police forces.

It was a different America then, one many Americans never knew or have forgotten. Most accepted the way things were, but not everyone. Change was in the air. You could sense it in the parks and in the talk of young black men. Black folks complained about housing discrimination, about being unable to vote. They weren't going to take it much longer. Something was stirring.

As a child, I sensed these things. Later, I heard and witnessed them. Still later, as a very young man, I played a role in them.

From the first time someone placed a basketball in my hands, all I ever really wanted to do was play ball. Basketball is the one part of my life in which I have always excelled. In basketball, I had no doubt or hesitation. In basketball, I was always among the best. So play ball is what I did, whenever and wherever I could. If you had told me then that someday I would be a part of history, that I would have a role in ending the segregation of America, I would have looked at you in stunned amazement. "All I want to do is play ball," I would have said.

And that night, the night when I played in the game "that changed everything," the night "the walls came tumbling down," "the night they drove old Dixie down," to name just some of the titles it's been given, I'd have answered with the same words: "All I want to do is play ball." But sometimes, even the simplest acts, ten men playing a game of ball they all love, can change a nation.

That memorable basketball season, that long winter and spring of glory and triumph, took place between the assassinations of President John F. Kennedy and Dr. Martin Luther King Jr. Our nation was fighting in Vietnam, and Muhammad Ali had refused to be drafted into the Army. In Mississippi, civil rights workers had been murdered, and it looked like the white men responsible would walk free. Just the year before, Dr. King had launched his drive to register black voters and was arrested along with 770 of his followers in Selma, Alabama, during a civil rights march. In the midst of the turmoil, Congress passed the Voting Rights Act.

At home, our small black and white television set held the images of white policemen unleashing snarling dogs on peaceful black protesters, their broad white faces spread wide in malevolent grins. Change was coming; the signs were everywhere. You could sense it in the gait of young blacks, hear it in the barber and beauty shop talk, and feel it in the pulse of many black Americans who demanded change. Blacks were standing up to racial injustice. They were no longer content to be treated as second-class citizens. It had begun slowly, but there was no turning back. What remained was the struggle.

During this time, my world was much smaller, and my concerns were more immediate. I grew up in the Sunnyside area of Houston, Texas, the city where I still live. More specifically, I grew up in inner-city black Houston. Eleven years before "the game," Rosa Parks refused to surrender her bus seat to a white man in Montgomery, Alabama, and launched the modern Civil Rights Movement. Just a year earlier, the U.S. Supreme Court had ruled in *Brown v. Board of Education of Topeka* that racial segregation in public schools was unconstitutional, but nobody had told that to anyone who mattered in Houston. There, segregation was alive and thriving, as it was across Texas and throughout the South. I attended all-black schools throughout high school, which, although good, were not equal to the white high schools in the same city. In elementary school, the only textbooks we had were white school discards. When the books were too torn up or too out of date for white kids, they were good enough for us.

I grew up as an only child, raised by my widowed mother, Elsie, who worked as the secretary at the local Southern Baptist church a few blocks from our house. It was a good, though not a prosperous, neighborhood with tree-lined paved streets and grass lawns. My dad died of heart disease when I was just six years old. I had a half brother, Roland, who was two years older than me. Growing up, he was more like a cousin than a brother, since he was raised in his mother's house across the city. He went to a different school but was a good friend and fine athlete, someone I sought to emulate. He also had a passion for the game of basketball, which inspired me. My six-foot, four-inch brother was the only player I ever saw who played guard, forward, and center very well. He played equally well on offense or defense.

To be a child in segregated Houston was to see and accept as normal, sights that today are unthinkable. I recall black and white water fountains. We had no car, and I remember sitting in the back of the bus with my mother. We would walk down the aisle, the white passengers never making eye contact, never looking us fully in the face, as if we were not people at all but some strange breed of intruders to be tolerated. The bus drivers were also white, because that was not a job for a "Negro." In the department stores where my mother and many other black women and families shopped, there were no black clerks, though the stores took our money gladly.

As I grew older, I knew there were black men with good jobs. There were black lawyers, teachers, postal workers, doctors, refinery workers, reporters, photographers, and entrepreneurs. Although my place in life did not have to be defined by my race, early on I knew that it would be easy to end up cutting grass for a living or laboring a lifetime in a menial job.

When I was old enough to understand such things, I heard that even the jails were segregated. Most police officers I saw in my neighborhood were white. There were a few black officers, but they could not arrest a white man. They could detain him but had to wait for a white officer to make the arrest.

When I was not at school or with my mom, I was at the Emancipation Park, about three blocks from our house. At the gym there, I sat with my friends and watched the big kids play basketball, considering these players to be the finest athletes there could possibly be. There was just one court and two baskets, so there was no option of us little kids getting a chance to play.

Also at the park was the community pool, where I spent a large portion of my childhood summers. One day I heard a pop like the backfire of a car, but the wave of excitement that swept through the young people in the pool and park told me this was no car. I ran with the others to the edge of the park, where we stood gawking at the crowd of white police officers who had taken up positions around the new local Black Panthers' headquarters.

I do not recall the details, just the images: the firing of tear gas and the sounds of gunfire as the men inside were cut down, the house catching fire and beginning to burn, the smell of the tear gas and of the smoke as it began to rise in the clear sky. Something terrible was happening.

My mother heard of the trouble and came running from the church, spotting me in the crowd where I stood gaping. She grabbed me and said, "We're going home. Now!"

I had no idea who The Black Panthers were and to this day do not know why the firefight took place. I just knew that white police officers had gunned down and burned young black men. There was something disturbing about that, a message there I could not articulate, but one that remained in my head for years.

Because I grew up in a segregated city, I had no white friends, no white classmates. The architects of the system, I suppose, intended for it to be that way. The idea was to keep the races apart, make certain we never learned we were all God's children with the same hopes, dreams, and needs. I existed and grew up in a racist bubble. It was years before I understood that racism touched me every day of my life, years before its ugly hand pressed me down and told me, "No, you can't have that, boy. Go away."

My childhood days were filled with the comforting warmth of my mom's love, the certainty of my school, the short walk to the church or park after school, the quiet evenings doing homework at the kitchen table as mom cooked dinner, perhaps an hour of television before going to bed.

> WE WERE ALL GOD'S CHILDREN WITH THE SAME HOPES, DREAMS, AND NEEDS.

Black and white television was mostly just white television. From time to time, I would see a black face. I would always say, "Look, Mom. There's one of us."

Houston was hot and muggy, but no one I knew had air conditioning. We opened the windows, ran the attic fan at night, and sweated a lot. It was the same for everybody, at least in black Houston. It was normal.

The church where my mother was secretary had several hundred parishioners. Every week, I attended service and Sunday school. As soon as I was old enough, I sang in the choir, as did my mother. Between prayer meetings, choir practice, and services, I was at church three nights a week. And in summer, there was Vacation Bible School on top of that. Mom kept me close, her only child, in her own safe world.

Because Mom was the church secretary, she received the calls about people needing help and was the one who responded. She cooked meals, took plates of food to people, offered them words of encouragement, saw to it they did not just vanish with no one caring. At night, she visited the sick in the hospital and saw to their needs as well. My mom's life was given to serving others. There are no words to properly express what a wonderful mother she was and what a wonderful child-hood she gave me.

My long days at the municipal pool had begun because of several family tragedies that had occurred in quick succession when I was six and seven years old. One summer day, there was a stir in the neighborhood, then the sounds of tramping feet, as a crowd rushed to a nearby bayou a mile from my house.

These bayous are all over Houston and in those days were much like the swamps you see in movies. I was not allowed to play near them, but my cousins, children of my father's sisters, not only played at the bayous—they swam in them.

Three times, I was part of the rush of people who hurried to join in the search for a missing cousin of mine. When the inevitable was accepted, heavy hooks were tossed into the murky water, and sweating men dragged them back and forth until finally they snagged a young body. They would pull my cousin onto the hot dirt, and we would stand there in silence.

It was shocking. The first time I saw a dead body, it was someone I loved lying unmoving and silent. My mother rushed up, clutched me close to her dress and in a low, firm voice that frightened me, said, "You're not going to drown. You're going to learn to swim." And so I did.

I attended seventh and eighth grade at Miller Junior High School. I tried out for the basketball team for the first time with some of my friends, and did not make it. The coach told us all to work out, to get stronger, and practice, practice, practice. He told us to go to Rice University and run the football stadium stairs every day all summer, to get in shape if we wanted to play ball.

I wanted to be like those players I had been watching at the park, so I took his words to heart—I was the only one cut from the team who did. Every day I rode my bike the six miles to Rice University and ran the stadium stairs. I would run until my sides ached, run until my legs were heavy and unresponsive, run until I was drenched in sweat and unable to move another muscle. I would rest and then run again. Afterwards, I would ride to the park, then sit in the gym and watch the big boys play. As I became more fit, I would sometimes get in an hour of practice, one hour before the gym was closed—the only time we little kids got to use the court.

Two schools were under construction, both of which would serve to determine my life course. For one year, during the ninth grade, I attended Attucks Junior High and this time made the team. The summer before, as I ran those stadium stairs, I grew six inches, to my full adult height of six feet, seven inches. I only weighed 185 pounds and was skinny as a stick, but I was taller than the rest and in far better shape. In school practice, I began to really learn the game, to use the advantage my size and quickness gave me. I learned to dribble, how to shoot, how to work the ball back and forth to create an opening. I also learned I had to hustle back on defense, to stop the fast break and to protect the basket.

Attucks won the city championship that year, and I was selected the best junior varsity player in Houston. That same year I held the record for the 50-yard dash, as it was then called. I was also city and district high school high jump champion, winning at the height of six feet, eight inches, losing to the guy who went on to win the state title. This was all a taste of what was to come.

At about this time, my mom bought a house, and we moved across town. Though the homes there were all new, this was a tough neighborhood, with black-on-black crime. Teenage gangs roamed the streets with chains in their back pockets, looking for fights. You had to carry a chain yourself and be ready to fight at a moment's notice.

The move meant that I would be attending the new Worthing High School. There, Coach Benny Roy put me on the B team, where I dominated the other, much smaller players. Lloyd Wells, who took the school photographs, worked for the local black newspaper, and was always on the lookout for new, young, black talent to spotlight. One day he visited the principal during practice. The principal told Lloyd that he just had to see a tall, lanky hot prospect who was going to be a real star for the new school. The men went to the gym, where the principal pointed me out.

Lloyd watched me scrimmage with the B team a few minutes then said, "Listen, you need to tell Coach Roy to get this guy off the B Team and onto the varsity. He can't get any better playing with the little guys."

When the principal spoke with the coach, he said I was not ready. Even though the season had already started, he was told to make the move regardless. I did not play much, but I learned a lot in practice, and that summer I started playing regularly at the city park.

For my two years of play as a starter on the varsity team at Worthing, I gained 35 pounds, but I was still thin for my height. My older, half brother attended Yates High School on the other side of town. As I started my varsity play, I wanted nothing so much as to emulate his play. Yates won the state championship that year, and my brother was selected as All-State.

Coach Roy was a great coach, one of the best. He worked us hard and emphasized offense. We scored many points, and that drew attention to both the team and to me. Otis Taylor played on that team and was great. Unfortunately, he left school in January and was not on our championship team. He later became an All-Pro wide receiver for the Kansas City Chiefs.

I QUICKLY LEARNED HOW UNSTOPPABLE IT WAS WHEN A BIG MAN MADE THE MOVE FOR THE BASKET.

Over those two years I really blossomed as a player, attracting more and more attention. Some of the best athletes at the park could dunk the ball, and by now so could I. I did not know it then, but this was a new development in the game. I quickly learned how unstoppable it was when a big man made the move for the basket. The simple act of stuffing the ball, jamming it into the basket, made a statement and was an act of intimidation.

My dream was to play college ball for my hometown team, the University of Houston Cougars. The local newspapers routinely featured high school players, and more and more often the articles included, or were about, me.

In 1962, Worthing downed Yates, 72-60 to win the 3-AAAA title. It was heady stuff for a brand new high school, heady stuff for me, who'd been part of the team, to beat my brother's former school. Playing center I scored 29 points, bringing my total points scored in high school to 790. During the tournament, playing in Jeppensen Field House, I fell one point short of tying the field house record when I scored 39 points. In a game against Madison from Dallas, we won the Negro AAAA crown in overtime. I was the leading scorer with 30 points.

The summer before my senior year, I was approached by Marvin Blumenthal, athletic director of the Houston Jewish Community Center. He asked me to play there. This was an opportunity only a select group of players received, and I knew it. Players such as Luke Jackson played, because the JCC served as a conduit for basketball players to Pan American University. It was there, that hot summer of 1962, that I first played ball against white athletes.

It was a first for some of them as well. I believe at least part of what Blumenthal was doing had nothing to do with finding players for integrated Pan American University. He had a greater agenda, and we were part of it.

That first integrated game, I did not know what to expect. Frankly, I questioned if the white boys could play very well. I quickly learned that white boys could play ball, too. Some of them were very, very good.

It was a good summer for me as a developing player. I learned a lot. Like all the gyms I knew in Houston, the building was not cooled. We left the doors and the high windows open as we played all day. I know I ate. I must have eaten, but I have no recollection of it. I arrived at ten in the morning, and we played until they shut the doors for the night.

The center was closed on Sunday, but that did not deter us. We went to the center, where one of us crawled to the high windows, pushed one open, and then stepped down to the folded seating to open the door for the rest. Without lights, except from the doors and windows, we played all day Sunday. We were intoxicated with basketball.

I took good care of myself. I ate right, got my rest, trained religiously. I was dead serious about my physical fitness, and I saw the results. My senior year I averaged 29 points a game, scoring a high of 48 in one game. In a game matched against Bubba Smith, I scored 43 points, the same number as my jersey. I was a unanimous choice for All-State and was named on several All-America high school teams, including *Dell Magazine, Basketball Illustrated,* and *Wilt Chamberlain's Basketball.* I was the first nationally recognized high school All-American from the state of Texas, black or white. What this meant was that I was the number one high school player in Texas and the most highly sought after player in the state.

I was also named to the West high school All-Star team, the first time players from the Gulf Coast met in a tournament. The headline in the newspaper was, "Latin [sic] Heads West Team." We dominated the East team, winning 62-50. I was named Most Valuable Player, scoring 16 points.

Later, the Texas legislature would pass a resolution honoring my career. It called me the "driving force" on my high school team, leading Worthing to its only state title. I was honored for having twice been named All-American. I averaged 29 points a game, with 19 rebounds, and 13 blocked shots.

College programs are made by recruiting star high school players, so I drew the attention of the coach for the University of Houston, Guy Lewis, who I estimate attended at least half of my high school games. We were very close, but it was not just him. That senior year I began receiving letters of inquiry from colleges and universities across the country. It seemed to me that my options were unlimited.

To be a star high school basketball player in Houston is to be a big man on what is a very small, but highly influential campus. I thought of myself as a winner and had always played on winning teams. I was a star, and I was treated as one everywhere I went—except at home. My mother had no interest in basketball, or in sports for that matter. Her life was the church and helping others. She never attended one of my games. I would come home excited and tell her how many points I had scored, how many shots I'd blocked, how many rebounds I got, and it meant nothing to her. She was glad we won, glad I had a good time—now what would I like for dinner?

But it wasn't possible for her to ignore my success entirely. Others would approach her with a grin, reach out to shake her hand, and ask how her boy was. Did she see him win that game the other night? As this started to become routine, slowly Mom came to realize that her son was considered to be a talented rising star with a great future ahead of him. The result was that it piqued her interest in basketball, but not in me as a player, because I was not on television. No, Mom's favorite player was someone else entirely.

There was not as much sports on television in those days. There was no cable or satellite television. We had three channels and a very limited number of hours of broadcasting. The National Basketball Association was not as big then as now, and I do not recall watching a single professional game. But, of course, the local University of Houston was on television.

Coach Guy Lewis was recruiting me heavily as I prepared to graduate from high school and had to make a choice about which college I would attend. The reality was that the UH sports program was segregated. Somewhere, in the back of my mind, I understood that. As the time came for me to go to college, and given the attention Coach Lewis invested in me, I was certain it would be integrated by the time I got there, or that I would be the player to integrate it.

"Change is coming," Coach Lewis would tell me. He wanted me to be ready for it. I was excited at the prospect, ready to cross that line. My dream was to stay home and attend the UH where I would be the star player. I would integrate the program, show them how the game was played, and be a hero.

That was how I imagined it, and for a while, it looked as though it might happen.

As graduation loomed, Coach Lewis began talking to me about attending a junior college first, then coming to the UH; integration was not going to happen in time for my freshman year. I vividly recall sitting on the bleachers at a UH game as he explained the realities of adult life to me. "They want to integrate the football program first. I cannot make a move until they do. I have tried, but there is just no way. Go to a junior college just one year. It is going to happen. Then I can bring you here."

He had it right, partially. I might have been raised in a segregated society, but I was a Houston man, I was a Texan. I wanted to play close to home, somewhere my play would be seen or known to my family and friends. I did not want to play with strangers. I wanted bragging rights on the playground.

All my life it had been my mother and me, so this was a big step for me. To go anywhere but UH meant leaving home. I was deeply disappointed, but I had known for at least a year that my dream might not happen. The pace of integration was moving so slowly, my career might very well race ahead. I was not going to wait. I told him I had no interest in attending a junior college and waiting for a program that could have me now, if only it would. I was better than that.

Playing before a hometown crowd, with the local newspapers and even my mom possibly coming to some of the games, just was not going to happen. As it turned out, it was not until 1964 that the UH Athletics Department integrated, with Elvin Hayes, Don Chaney, and Warren McVey in the football program.

I had been receiving inquiries from all over the country, as far away as UCLA and NYU, so on the surface I was not concerned about picking a college. Many of the inquiries came from segregated white universities that didn't know I was black. I got a kick out of that. One of them was Vanderbilt, located in Nashville, as was all-black Tennessee State. All these schools knew was that I was a high school All-American, and they wanted to take the first step in recruiting me. I estimate I received 300 inquiry letters altogether.

Since UH was closed to me, and because I wanted to stay home, or at least close to home, my choices were limited. This was the plight of black basketball players—still not widely understood. Most could play at the big-city Catholic universities or at traditionally black schools, but that was it. If you were from the South and wanted to play in the South, your choices were very limited. The consequence was that many gifted athletes never played beyond high school and simply vanished. Who knows how many great stars were buried in menial jobs? Though occupied with basketball, I now understood what all those marches were about, why so many people risked the attack dogs, sniper fire, and jail.

This was when I came to understand the implications of racism and the fundamental injustice of it. I knew something was wrong with a system that kept some of the best players out of certain schools because of their race. I really believed that my hometown school, the University of Houston, would make an exception for me. What I learned was that Texas Western, [now the University of Texas at El Paso,] and Pan American were the only two schools in Texas recruiting black athletes for integrated programs.

THIS WAS MY FIRST REALIZATION THAT, AS A YOUNG BLACK MAN, MY HORIZONS WERE NOT LIMITLESS.

I was slowly coming of age, figuring it out for myself. It was all coming together: limited opportunities, fewer choices, and what options might actually exist. This was my first realization that, as a young black man, my horizons were not limitless. Here I was, nationally identified as the best basketball player in my home state, one of the best in the country, and I had to manage my entry into college ball as if I were an adult plotting a career path. That's what I was doing, and I was growing up very fast.

CHAPTER 3

JUDGE

He taught us everything.
He taught us to work hard,
to expect more in life, to be men.
TEXAS WESTERN'S DAVID LATTIN

THOUGH MY FATHER WAS dead and my mother was busy supporting us, I wasn't alone. From the first time he saw me playing at Worthing High School, local newspaper reporter and photographer Lloyd Wells took an interest in me. I came to learn that he knew talent when he saw it, but most of all he knew commitment, hard work, and a willingness to pay the price for success. Later, I learned his interest wasn't just in black athletes. He lent a hand to young black teens who went on to become doctors, lawyers, and university academics as well.

Lloyd was the hardest-working man I ever knew. He was a cheerleader and a one-man public relations operation for the black community. Lloyd saw to it that we young black athletes received state and national attention. He took us under his wing, nurtured us, showed us the value of hard work, and turned us into men.

For generations, African-Americans had been finding ways to improve their assigned lot in American life. Some founded Negro colleges and others gained entrance to once all-white colleges and universities, all the while systematically working their way into the professions. Others achieved through athletics. As they succeeded, many looked around to help others of the race, to slowly pull us all up. It was an impulse, indeed an obligation, most successful blacks acted on.

I have no doubt that Worthing High School came about as a result of their efforts and those of white people of good will who knew injustice when they saw it and were willing to create change. Black entertainers were just starting to boycott cities and states which refused to let them perform before integrated audiences. Sammy Davis Jr., one of the Rat Pack on stage, wasn't allowed to eat in the restaurant of the Las Vegas hotel where they performed or stay in the same quality rooms until Frank Sinatra and the others made an issue of it. Nat King Cole drove long distances across the Old Confederacy, unable to use the restrooms of the gas stations that sold him gas, forced to take rooms in homes from kind strangers in cities where there were no hotel rooms for any African-American. Jackie Robinson had broken the color barrier in baseball, and the walls were falling, though slowly, in the National Football League and the National Basketball Association. Every professional black athlete who "made it" was a hero and was heavily promoted in the black community. I don't think it is too much to say that these men meant more to black Americans than similar white stars did to white Americans.

There were, as well, black newspapers that catered to an African-American readership and wrote about issues important to us. Lloyd Wells worked for at least two of these, the *Houston Informer* and the *Forward Times,* Houston's leading black newspaper.

The only vacations Lloyd took were with us, his "league," his "sons" as he called us. On weekends he drove us in perennially new cars, usually a Cadillac, to Galveston, where he laid out a huge lunch and we spent the day hanging out at the beach. The group included, among many others, Bubba Smith, Willie Ray Smith, John Brisker, Otis Taylor, Warren McVey, and Phil Harris. There was also Willie Baker, Skull, Graden, Boney, Avery, C-Boy, and myself.

Somewhere along the line people started calling Lloyd "The Judge." His friend Gene Kilroy says it was Lloyd who called others "Judge" first and they gave him the name in return. I never learned the reason behind it. It was "Judge" here, "Judge" there. When he died in 2005, it was "the Judge" who was laid to rest.

Lloyd was very flamboyant, a great dresser. He loved the color red. In fact, any color we in his "league" thought too garish or extreme was just right with him. If he spotted a shirt he especially liked, why off we went to find one just like it, or one even brighter, and whichever one of us was with him that day came away with a new shirt as well.

Lloyd was a trailblazer, a man ahead of his time. Not one to follow, he always took a new path. He was a great talker, and you couldn't not listen. But he wasn't just a talker, he was a doer. I never knew a man who worked harder. "If you want something done, give it to a busy man," he would say. He told me, over and over, that for all my talent and size, I'd never make it if I didn't apply myself. I had to work hard. I had to study, too, because I might get injured. I had to expect failure along the way, because that's how life could be. He walked tall and taught us to do the same. He was that kind of man.

Lloyd Wells was in his late 30's when he first saw me, and I first got to know him. He was six feet tall, weighed 215. He had served twice in the Marine Corps, the first time seeing combat in the Pacific. He attended Southern University in Baton Rouge, Louisiana on an athletic scholarship. After World War II, he moved to Houston and attended Houston College for Negroes (now Texas Southern University), where he was the first athlete to letter in football, basketball, and track. With the outbreak of the Korean War, he reenlisted and was wounded near the Chosin Reservoir and received the Purple Heart. He suffered a permanent hearing loss thereafter.

Lloyd went on to serve as commissioner of one of the semi-pro football leagues organized by Hank Stram. He became the first black full-time scout for the Kansas City Chiefs football team of the American Football League. At that time, there was fierce competition with the rival NFL, and Lloyd snatched more than one fine black ballplayer just about to sign an NFL contract to sign a better one with the Chiefs.

When the University of Houston wanted to recruit Warren McVey for their football program, they had no way of getting him, because McVey was going to Kansas. Someone told the UH coach that if he could get Lloyd Wells on the case, he could deliver McVey, and that's how they got him.

When Lloyd was working for the Kansas City Chiefs, the American League football team desperately wanted to sign Otis Taylor, but he was scheduled to ink a contract with the Dallas Cowboys. Lloyd had known Otis since he'd been a student at

Worthing High School, and he was one of the "league." He learned the hotel where Otis was sequestered, safe from the grasp of the AFL, then found a way to reach him through a window. Within minutes Otis was out that same window and in a private jet to Kansas City, where he signed a lucrative deal with the Chiefs. Without Lloyd, the Chiefs would not have appeared in the first Super Bowl, and they would not have won in 1969, with Otis Taylor leading the team.

Hank Stram, head football coach of the Chiefs at that time, said, "Lloyd was one of the main reasons we were in the first Super Bowl and won the fourth one. He was out of sight. Without him, we wouldn't make it."

When Lloyd was still with the Chiefs, after they were in the new, combined NFL, he met Gene Kilroy, and they became inseparable friends. "He was a man of three D's: dedicated, determined, and disciplined," Gene said. "He was a seeker of talent. Not only did he seek, he brought it back."

Gene worked in the home office of the Philadelphia Eagles at the time and went on to a decades-long career with nearly every Las Vegas hotel, promoting highly successful sports events. "He was like a brother," Kilroy said. "He would come to Las Vegas to see me many times, and I lived in his home in Houston's fifth ward on Chew Street. Many times I would meet people and tell them I lived in that part of Houston, and they thought I was lying, because white people didn't live there. But with him and me, it wasn't about color or race. It was about two men who genuinely cared about each other." Gene says that Lloyd mixed with kings yet walked with the poor. Frank Sinatra and John Kennedy Jr. both loved him. "Where's the Judge?" they'd ask whenever they saw Gene.

Gene told me how Lloyd had talked to Hank Stram about scouting for him to get black players into the NFL, and Hank gave him the go-ahead. In the NFL, if you sign a free agent who makes your team, they look at you as a hero. Lloyd signed eight that made All-Pro. He was a tremendous asset to the Kansas City Chiefs, and Hank loved him. When Hank left, Lloyd resigned. He didn't want to be there with another coach and a new regime.

He called Gene and told him of his decision. He was already close with him and Ali, so Gene brought him to the training camp where he put Ali through calisthenics. This was in 1977. Lloyd was well loved and had great sense of humor. Most of all, he was committed to Ali. You can't buy loyalty—you either have it or you don't—and Lloyd had loyalty. Muhammad Ali hired Lloyd as his business manager. It was a long, long association.

In the 1966 movie *Muhammad Ali—The Whole Story*, Lloyd played himself as one of the great boxer's photographers. Later, Lloyd worked with Tommy "Hit Man" Hearns, George Foreman, and Mustafa Muhammad. With all these fighters, he taped their workouts and made suggestions as they watched them together. He had an uncanny eye when it came to athletics.

In 1983, Lloyd was featured in *Sports Illustrated*. He'd already appeared in many other publications by then. In 1993, he was presented with the

YOU CAN'T BUY LOYALTY—YOU EITHER HAVE IT OR YOU DON'T.

Outstanding Texan Award in Sports by the Texas Legislative Black Caucus. Two years before his death, Lloyd was inducted into the African-American Ethnic Sports Hall of Fame.

Lloyd set another example for his "league" with his fine clothes, flashy new cars, and winning personality.

One of his major contributions to black youths was to organize multiracial All-Star teams of high school basketball players. I had played in one of those competitions. These games served to showcase black athletes who in earlier times would simply have vanished after graduating from high school. Through his efforts, they could be seen playing against the best white players, and there was no question of their ability. I can't even count how many played in college on an athletic scholarship, obtained a degree, and went on to a better life. If he couldn't raise enough money to support the tournaments, it came out of his own pocket.

At the time Lloyd was encouraging me, he decided to end segregated seating at Houston Colt .45 (later renamed the Houston Astros) major league baseball games and wrote a series of columns condemning the practice. The way it worked was that black fans crawled through a hole in the back fence. That's right, they crawled into the game, bought a ticket, and got to sit in the "rear of the bus."

Lloyd thought it was disgusting. He went down to the hole and told African-Americans there that from now on they would go in the front gates and sit where they wanted or they weren't going in at all. He would take the picture of anyone who knelt down to crawl through that hole and put it on the front page of the *Forward Times*. His repeated presence created such a stir that he was arrested for disturbing the peace, but it worked. The hole was closed and black folks walked through the front gates just like everybody else who bought a ticket.

When I graduated from Worthing in January, 1963, I was being recruited by hundreds of schools across the nation. My own preference, the University of Houston, wasn't available to me because I'd been born the "wrong" color. There were all-black colleges that would have taken me in a heartbeat, and there were integrated schools nationwide that wanted me, but my intention was to stay near home. I might have been six feet, seven inches tall, weighed more than 230 pounds, and been a big man on a high school campus, but I'd never been away from home or my mother's cooking before.

Recruitment rules were complicated then, as I'm sure they are now. Expenses for campus visits were paid by the schools, but I could only fly to four colleges. I had to drive to the rest, and I recall there was a limit on how many times I could visit a college; three, I think it was. Altogether, I visited some fourteen colleges and universities that summer, and Lloyd drove me to all of them, mostly in his brand new, red Ford Lincoln Continental convertible. It was the model where the rear doors opened and closed from the rear so that the four door handles were clustered together. I can see that car today as if I had just stepped out of it. I can still smell the rich leather and hear Lloyd's voice as we talked about everything, and I mean everything, except the colleges we were visiting. We did that once we got there. What a summer.

Tennessee State, where Lloyd had a good friend in Coach Harold Hunter, and Wichita State in Kansas, were the farthest away. I also went to distant West Texas State and Oklahoma City. I could have played for UCLA in a heartbeat, but that was the other side of the country. It might just as well have been China as far as I was concerned.

Certain colleges with great basketball programs were simply not available to me for the same reason the UH wasn't. The all-white University of Kentucky had won more national championships than any college in history, four, but there was no question of going there. It was the same with Duke. If I wanted to go to school in the South, my options were limited. I could try to find one of the few integrated programs or attend an all-black college. That was it.

By and large these campus visits went well and were an eye-opener for me. At nearly every college, I was assured by the coach that I would get the ball. I was averaging 29 points a game in high school, and they told me I would get that same chance with them. They would craft the game to my advantage. In other words, they were promising I would be the star. They'd see to that with the style of ball they were going to play. This was pretty heady stuff for an 18-year-old kid.

But being young and talented, I wasn't letting this be as simple as it could be. There were a number of friends from the neighborhood who were good football players, but for all the success of Worthing's basketball team, our football team had a bad season. Good as they were, no college was showing an interest in them, and without an athletic scholarship, none of them were going to attend college. I promised them that any school that wanted me had to take them, and throughout my recruitment summer, that was part of the deal—one not well received at times.

It was clear to me that Lloyd preferred I attend Tennessee State, and the school was willing to give scholarships to my friends, but there was an integrated college in the far corner of my home state, Texas Western, whose coach was heavily recruiting me. Lloyd made it clear that he considered Texas Western a second choice, but one worth a visit. At first, I thought it too far away to even consider, but as other distant colleges entered the mix, it didn't seem that distant, after all. Anyway, one of my heroes, Jim "Bad News" Barnes, played there, and this would be a chance to meet him. How could I say no?

Don Haskins was the relatively new coach at unheralded Texas Western. He'd recruited "Bad News" Barnes out of junior college, and his play had served to put Texas Western on the map. Coach Haskins wrote in his book that he had first learned about Barnes from a college teammate who'd coached him at Cameron Junior College in Oklahoma.

Barnes was being heavily recruited by a number of big-name schools, and he was going to be difficult to land for any of them, but especially for a college as obscure as Texas Western. Coach Haskins told him what he had to offer, how a player of his talent would stand out and not be one of several great players on a team, how he could put Texas Western on the map, and in doing so make a great name for himself. Still, Barnes was undecided, so when Coach Haskins found him practicing free throws in the gym, he challenged him to a free throwing contest in front of his teammates.

Now, I personally doubt there is a college player in America who believes his coach can beat him on the court at anything. You might respect your coach, perhaps even know his own career record, but the coach, compared to you, is an old, slow guy. There is no way he can be better than you. Coach Haskins actually had very little to lose since it was unlikely Barnes would sign with him, and he was a great free throw shooter. Barnes accepted, and the pair agreed to rules. They each would shoot 25 times and the one with the most buckets won. Coach Haskins shot first and hit all twenty-five. Like I said, he was a great free throw shooter. Barnes missed his second and third attempts and signed with Texas Western. What else could he do?

Barnes was a big man with the kind of natural athleticism you now associate with big basketball players, but it was rare then. He had been recruited by Cameron Junior College while still playing high school ball in Arkansas. He and his whole family moved to Stillwater, Oklahoma. There he led the Stillwater High School team to an undefeated season with 20 wins. The next year, he carried a less-than-talented team to the state high school championship.

Barnes was simply a great sign for Coach Haskins. He led the Texas Western Miners to two unprecedented NCAA tournament appearances. Coach Haskins wrote that he thought they had a genuine shot at winning it all that second year but were eliminated in the second round.

When I went to the Texas Western campus, I had plenty of time to visit with Barnes. I had a chance to see him play in person and was very impressed. Frankly, my visit was about basketball. I never looked at the buildings, the campus, or the dorm where I would be living. Instead, I looked at the basketball court where I would be playing.

Barnes and I talked about a lot of things, what his plans were after college, if he would play professional ball. Barnes talked about how happy he was there, how glad he was he'd selected the school. He told me that El Paso was a great place for basketball because the college was the center for the city. There was nothing else to do and no professional sports teams to compete.

He also liked the people in El Paso, had enjoyed the surroundings, and believed that Coach Haskins was a winning coach. In his time there they'd taken great care of him. He encouraged me to attend. He said that I could play my kind of game; that is, an offense set around the center getting the ball.

At this time, the Texas Western student body was 50 percent white and 49 percent Hispanic, while the only blacks were the athletes or a handful of students whose parents were at Fort Bliss. There were a lot of locals, but a significant number of students came from all over the country. I liked what I saw and what I heard, but El Paso was a long, long way from home.

Coach Haskins wrote later that, with Barnes's departure, he knew he was going to need a big man for the 1965-66 season and had his eye on me as a replacement. He had driven across the state of Texas to watch me play my senior year, in itself a feat that impressed me. He also saw me play in one of Lloyd's showcase tournaments; one I dominated.

I'm told he can still recall my home telephone number since he called me so many times after games to talk to me. Coach Haskins later said he was impressed with my toughness, not just my physique. He watched me work the mental part of the game, the part where you win through intimidation, without having to actually do anything. When you crash the boards and the other players are afraid to go up with you, you've already won. He liked that about me. Heck, I liked that about me. That's why I cropped my hair short and grew a mustache, trying to show the opposition they were playing against someone who was already a man.

I knew I had a role to play, bigger than up the middle. I would not agree to attend any college that would not offer scholarships to four of my high school classmates, who incidentally were football players and very good athletes. Being one of the best high school basketball players in the country, I felt my college choices, albeit limited, would afford me an opportunity to make a stand and get scholarships for all of us. I later called my position the "The Real Deal"—all five of us or none of us.

> I LATER CALLED
> MY POSITION
> THE "THE REAL
> DEAL"—ALL FIVE OF
> US OR NONE OF US.

I said I'd come to Texas Western, but only if my football friends also got scholarships. Hearing about this, Coach Haskins called just to be sure he had heard it right. "David," he said, "I'm just recruiting you." Coach Haskins obviously did not think much of the "The Real Deal." As bad as he wanted me, once he realized that I was serious about bringing my four classmates, my door shut there.

But I was not deterred. I became even more determined to fulfill my commitment to my classmates. Something in my soul and spirit told me I had to make this stand, not only for them, but also for other deserving, black, student athletes who had no other college options without a scholarship. If I didn't stick to my convictions and bring these guys with me, they would be out in the cold.

I knew that segregation and racial discrimination would keep us down forever if we did not break the choke hold. I wanted myself and other black, student athletes to have a college education and the opportunity to not only better ourselves and our communities, but also live The American Dream.

Years later, I was told that it took a young warrior (me) on and off the basketball court to join in with the seasoned and determined to help win victories one battle at a time, by fighting the good fight for racial equality. Thank God, I was one of the best high school players in the country; it allowed me to speak and be heard when I said, "We deserve an education. Let us in."

Lloyd passed in September, 2005. What a man. He was with me when I signed my first professional contract. He was with me when I bought my first car, a Cadillac like his that year, of course. I was honored to be one of his pallbearers, joined by Tommy Hearns, Gene Kilroy, and others. At his funeral, in tribute I wore a bright red shirt. I spoke of us, his "surrogate sons," and how, when others called us "boys," he made us men.

CHAPTER 4

THE BARON

The man was a genius. He won with little players, big players, and middle-sized players. He won with talented players and untalented players.

KENTUCKY PLAYER RALPH BEARD

BASKETBALL WASN'T ALWAYS THE athletic, graceful game we are accustomed to seeing today. Invented as a sport to be played indoors on volleyball courts, it was at first slow and very physical—at one point considered to be more violent than football. All that changed, primarily through the efforts of one man—Adolph Rupp.

Rupp, still considered by many to have been the greatest college basketball coach of all time, was born in Halstead, Kansas. The town itself had just 1,200 residents. It was an all-white community with the kind of ordinance common in the region at the time; no blacks were allowed to spend the night.

His Kentucky Wildcats team enjoyed success from his first season on. At the time of his retirement, Rupp had the most wins of any coach in the game with an unprecedented four National Championships. In forty-two years as head coach, he lost on average fewer than five games a season.

Ballhandling, action, and excitement were the hallmarks of a Rupp basketball team, a style called Racehorse Basketball.

This fast style of play was an immediate success. It was a style that influenced the game nationwide as Kentucky enjoyed greater and greater success with it. Kentucky went 15-3 that first year with him and never had a losing season as long as he was coach.

His teams were not only well disciplined on the court, but also generally better conditioned than his opponents. Rupp recruited players for quickness, and he coached his teams to use the fast break, augmented with quick outside jump shots whenever possible. He coached the use of inside screens to set up shots and had his players establish a practiced offense. He introduced the style of play that we follow today, and for that reason, if no other, we all owe him a great deal.

But the key to his success might very well have been his recruiting. He would read up on the high scorers in high school, then, in the early days at least, go visit them. He would take the youngster out and buy him the biggest steak he could find. If the teenager picked at it or made a fuss, he'd forget him, but if he dived into the meat with gusto, as if he'd never had a full meal in his life, Rupp would sign the boy then and there. He knew hunger when he saw it, having experienced so much of it himself, and he knew that kind of hunger would extend to how a boy played the game.

A racist incident occurred in Lexington, which only reinforced the city's national reputation. In 1959, Temple's integrated basketball team had flown to the city to face Kentucky at the Memorial Coliseum. The black principal of Lexington's Dunbar High School and the school's black coach were given highly prized courtside seats. A volunteer Boy Scout, having never seen black men in such a prestigious location, told the pair they had to move. The men displayed their tickets, and the Kentucky athletic director was sent for to settle the issue. The men were told to change seats, but rather than create a stir and possibly jeopardize their jobs, the men left the game.

A well-publicized incident occurred two years later when the Boston Celtics and St. Louis Hawks of the NBA came to Lexington for a game. Two former Wildcats were on the teams, one to each, and the game was a sellout. The Celtics stayed downtown at the Phoenix Hotel, and on game day Bill Russell along with other African-American players from his team were refused service in the hotel's dining room. They flew home and did not play.

Adolph Rupp has been vilified as a racist. I wouldn't know. What I can say is that there were then and are today people who believe in white superiority, and not just on the basketball court. Those were views widely held by many whites in America at that time, but more importantly, our nation was changing; doors that had always been closed were opening. Few men get to carve out their own place in history. Rupp was one of them.

By the early 1960s, many Southern schools and conferences began to integrate. In 1963, Kentucky had a president who wanted to integrate the university, including its athletic programs, but by the 1965-66 season it had not occurred. Rupp's quest for a fifth title with an all-white team was on a collision path with a team from Texas Western who had something to prove—something, as it turned out, a lot more significant than just winning a tournament.

The 1964-65 Wildcats fell to a 15-10 record, the worst in Rupp's then 36 years at Kentucky. It had left a bitter taste in his mouth, and he was determined to undo the blot on his record. At 64 years of age, there was talk that his glory years were behind him, and that perhaps it was time for him to move aside and turn the job over to a younger, more energetic man. Rupp surely felt the heat.

For the 1965-66 season, Rupp had an excellent core of four fine players remaining on the team on which to build. Unfortunately, not one was any taller than six feet, five inches. They remained on campus that summer, practicing, feeling the sting of the bad season the year before. As a result, they were closely bonded.

There was Tommy Kron, a guard, who was expecting a successful new season, even though they'd had injuries the previous year; and Rupp had been absent on occasion, suffering from inflamed veins in his legs.

Also staying on campus to prepare for the new season was Larry Conley, who roomed with Kron, as well as Pat Riley and Louie Dampier, both talented juniors. The four held their own practices, studied together, and socialized. They held pickup games several times a week. As the season approached, they took part in a new conditioning program designed by one of Rupp's assistant coaches, consisting of a rigorous running regimen along with weight conditioning. Running days were alternated with weight training. One player found the schedule so daunting that he regularly lost his lunch. Conley later said of the regimen, "It damn near killed us."

Until then, it had been assumed that playing the game hard in practice developed the right muscles and stamina needed for games. It was thought that excess running would wear a player out and that weight lifting was counterproductive, as it developed bulky muscles. All that was being reexamined in sports at the time, and this season Rupp decided to act on the new approach to competitive basketball. It was unlike the previous seasons, strenuous and demanding in ways playing basketball for him previously had not been.

> IT WAS UNLIKE THE PREVIOUS SEASONS, STRENUOUS AND DEMANDING IN WAYS PLAYING BASKETBALL FOR HIM PREVIOUSLY HAD NOT BEEN.

Because of the relatively diminutive size of his star players, Rupp decided it was going to be a running season for the Wildcats. Emphasis would be placed on quick ball handling and the fast break to create open jump shots or to set up a pass inside the defense.

Rupp was satisfied with the team play he found with this collection of players. Atypically for one of his teams, this kind of cohesion had been lacking the previous year when individual play had taken over self-sacrifice for the team. The leader of their team was six feet, three inch Pat Riley, who went on to the NBA and fame as an NBA coach. From New York State, he possessed a certain street toughness the others might have lacked. He was not intimidated by Rupp in the least.

Tommy Kron, at six feet, five inches, was a fine defender, lanky and tall for a guard at the time. Kentucky played a 1-3-1 defense on occasion, which placed a great deal of pressure on the young man. He put up with Rupp's comments, just so he played.

Louie Dampier was just six feet tall but the team's best shooter. He'd led the team in scoring the previous year with 17 points a game. He was adept at using the Wildcats' screen to cover his jump shots. He had lost both his parents as a teenager and tended towards a sad demeanor.

Larry Conley was the fourth returning player. He was six feet, three inches in height, and a consummate team player. He'd met Rupp years earlier when he'd first decided he was going to play ball for Kentucky, and following a hard-fought victory, he had impulsively hugged the aloof coach.

The Wildcats were aggressive on the boards, could shoot and play defense, and passed the ball unselfishly. What Rupp lacked was a tall dominant center, and that could easily have been a fatal flaw in an otherwise fine team. Rupp selected 230-pound, six feet, five inch sophomore Thad Jaracz for the role, despite his lack of height. "We've got to have somebody," Rupp said. "That guy's got some possibilities." Despite his bulk, Jaracz was quick and difficult to guard.

These were the starters of the team that would be called Rupp's Runts. They were, Rupp confessed, his favorite team of all. There were two players who came in regularly off the bench. They were six feet, eight inch Cliff Berger who could play inside, though he was not agile, and Bobby Tallent, a fine outside shooter.

Practice was at three-fifteen and was all business. Rupp attended in white tennis shoes, crisp tan cotton pants, and a white shirt, his whistle hung about his neck. Free throw practice was followed by position shooting, this occupying the first three-quarters of an hour in silence except for the bounce of the ball, the wobble of the basket, and the squeak of the shoes on the highly polished court. "No one is to speak unless he can improve on the silence," Rupp instructed at the beginning of each season.

RUPP RAN A TIGHT SHIP, BUT HE PRODUCED WINNERS. FOR THAT, THE YOUNG MEN WERE PREPARED TO OVERLOOK A GREAT DEAL.

This was practice by the numbers, motivated primarily by fear. Make a mistake and Rupp blew his whistle or shouted at you, his comments often sarcastic and demeaning. There were players who could not take the incredible pressure this style of coaching created and transferred out of the program. There was no jostling, no laughter, no fun. It was all grim work.

Next, Rupp gathered his players at center court and in a long soliloquy delivered his evaluation of what he'd just seen and instructions on what they were to do next. He remained distant from his players, leaving close contact and discussion to his assistants. The speech was followed by an hour of drills Rupp wanted. Every practice was exactly one hour and 45 minutes long. They were designed to improve the basics, maintain sharpness, and get the players accustomed to their rhythm with one another.

That season, Rupp went further than he ever had before. Besides the running and weight training, he held two practices a day. The second session began at nine at night. His purpose was to teach the team a new offense. He believed his old one had grown stale and that teams too easily prepared for it. This new one was to be available if the old one wasn't working.

Rupp might have loved his boys, but he was hard on them. The players alternately hated and respected Rupp. He ran a tight ship, but he produced winners. For that, the young men were prepared to overlook a great deal.

Every player on the Kentucky team had played against black opponents at some point. It was not their decision to keep the program all white. For the twenty-seven regular season games the Wildcats played they faced less than twelve African-American opponents. Riley later said, he'd never seen a basketball dunked before; he didn't know it could even be done.

That memorable 1965-66 season, the Wildcat team averaged better than 84 points a game. When traveling, they donned matching blazers. Riley later recalled that season up to the final game as the most glorious time of his life, and so it might very well have been for Rupp.

The 1966 championship game was to have been his fifth title. It was, instead, the first and only time he was defeated in the championship game. It has become the game that has established his legacy.

CHAPTER 5

EL PASO

*If there is anyplace in the world where
I was treated as a first class person,
it's El Paso, Texas. Without a doubt,
it has the nicest, friendliest, warmest
people you ever saw in your life.*

TEXAS WESTERN'S DAVID LATTIN

THE COACH OF THE 1966 NCAA Championship Basketball team, my coach, was Don Haskins. Coach Haskins had received a great deal of credit for what we accomplished, and he deserved it. What he did should not have been a big deal at the time, but it was. He went out and recruited the best player for each position he could find, regardless of color. And when it came time to play a game, he put the best five players on the court, regardless their race. This is so commonplace today it is hard to imagine there was a time in America when it was revolutionary, but it was.

In 1962, Coach Haskins' second year at Texas Western, he received letters of complaint because he was playing too many black players. One of his black athletes complained that he entered the game off the bench when he should have been a starter. The coach showed him a stack of letters and asked him to read them. When the player looked up from the unabashed racism written there, Coach Haskins said, "You know, one day

I'm going to be able to play my best players." By 1965, he decided that time had come.

In the 1960's, Middle America was largely undecided on what to do about race. For most Americans, it wasn't an issue they faced in their daily life. "Outside agitators" were routinely blamed by Southern sheriffs for the violence associated with marches, and the rest of America was inclined to agree. Blacks were fine to clean your house or cut your grass but were generally considered unable to do much else. Deed restrictions or local ordinances kept African-Americans from owning property in white neighborhoods. In all professional sports, the dominant race was white. The failure of a black team to win at all in college basketball was simply considered normal.

For African-Americans, it was a matter of "knowing your place." Many older black Americans were uncertain of the wisdom of the Civil Rights Movement, fearing gains already made could be lost. Out of sight, out of mind was expected behavior—and not just at work or in segregated neighborhoods; white America dominated television and movies. Whenever an African-American appeared on television, it was not uncommon for the family to rush to the set to see one of "our" people. The mere presence of black faces on television was a moment of significance.

In the 1960's, when it came to race and basketball, there existed an unwritten rule. While there were integrated teams across the country, though very few in the South, they never, or almost never, played five black players at the same time. The idea was that if a coach ever did that, the game would disintegrate into some kind of street brawl. What was needed was one or two white boys on the court at all times, like over-seers, to make sure the other boys played the way they were supposed to. The system was called, believe it or not, the "quota," and it was a popular subject among white coaches. What's your quota? How many can you put on at the same time? How many can you recruit? Everyone knew what they were talking about.

This "quota" system translated into two black players on the court at home, three on the road, four only if you were behind, never five black players at the same time, for appearance's sake. The style of ball that had evolved in inner-city pickup games was not to become the collegiate style, and there was a great deal of attention paid to the message the game was conveying to society as a whole.

CHANGE IS ALWAYS DIFFICULT.

When it comes to integration, I have a theory that runs a bit counter to the usual explanation. The customary story goes that the schools were integrating their teams slowly, not wanting to offend a largely white fan base, or cause trouble when they played all-white teams in the South. It goes on to suggest that black athletes played a different style of ball, one that went against teamwork, and that a certain ratio of black to white had to be maintained to preserve the game as it was meant to be.

I suppose there might be some truth to the first, since change is always difficult. My experience has been that most people, black and white, are not racists; actual racists make up a small segment of any group. It might be vocal, and because it makes its presence known, that small group might seem bigger than it is, but the actual racists are a small minority.

To my way of thinking, there really wasn't much reason to move so slowly. Fans want to win. Period. Skin color doesn't mean much when a coach produces winning teams.

What I think was really going on was that white coaches, white athletic directors, even many white fans, feared that black athletes were *better* than white ones. I've played against some really fine white players, some better than me, though I wouldn't admit it at the time, and I've played against not-so-good black players. There are great, and not great, players in both races. What I will say is that I believe black athletes brought a level of athleticism to the game that had been lacking, one all players, of all races, aspire to emulate.

In the 1960's, when it came to race and college basketball, it was pretty simple. There were coaches in parts of the country who wanted to maintain a status quo of white supremacy on the basketball court, and there were coaches like Don Haskins who weren't out to make a point about race. They just wanted to win.

The same year that Rupp was hired as head coach at the University of Kentucky, Don Haskins was born in Enid, Oklahoma. His dad had been a fine athlete and supported the family as a truck driver. Coach Haskins loved sports from the start, but his first choice was baseball, a game at which he excelled as a young man. He played semi-pro ball after high school but fate, or destiny if you will, kept pulling him towards basketball. He'd played a lot of basketball, along with baseball, in high school and learned the jump shot, a real innovation in the game, at an early age.

Coach Haskins attended Oklahoma A&M under legendary coach Henry Iba, whose son he later hired as an assistant coach. He was mostly a bench warmer in college and wrote later that he hated Iba as did the other players at the time, but he studied how the man coached, and Coach Haskins believes that's what made him the coach he became.

A lesson he took from his senior year had an impact on our championship season. Oklahoma A&M was one of the teams favored to win the NCAA championship. The team had had a very good year and the players were cocky and overconfident, certain they could defeat anyone. Then, in postseason play, they lost to the University of Kansas in triple overtime. This was a team they had beaten badly just two weeks earlier. Kansas went on to lose in the championship game by one point.

After college, Coach Haskins played professional Amateur Athletic Union basketball, making more than he'd have made in the NBA at the time. The way it worked was that a company sponsored an AAU team and put you on the payroll or arranged to get you a job elsewhere. That way the games were technically amateur, though the players were making good money from their sponsors. Haskins visited El Paso his first time playing AAU ball, competing against a group of Army veterans from nearby Fort Bliss.

Coach Haskins' first coaching job was for Benjamin High School, where he also coached football, girls basketball, and drove the bus. Not knowing how to coach football, he later wrote, he settled on yelling a lot, Mr. Iba style. He depended on his assistant to teach technique.

Coach Haskins coached other high school basketball teams with success, then in 1961, was hired as basketball coach at Texas Western. He and his family were to live in an apartment at the dormitory and eat for free in the cafeteria, if they wanted, and part of his job was to maintain the rules and keep order in the dormitory. He was thirty-one years old.

At that time, Texas Western had a student body of just seven thousand. It was an obscure college in a remote corner of Texas. I had initially learned about the school because it and Pan American were the only integrated colleges in Texas. Still, El Paso was a college town, and basketball was *the* sport. Though the African-American population was less than one percent, the black athletes were generally welcome in ways they weren't in Houston. The culture was by history quite tolerant of race. Anglos and Mexicans had been mixing there for generations, and if there was any racial tension, it was between those groups. Nearby Fort Bliss had black soldiers, and throughout World War II and afterwards they had been entertained in El Paso and nearby Juarez, Mexico.

This is not to say that Coach Haskins wasn't put under pressure to avoid playing too many blacks at the same time. Perception was still viewed as important, and there was apparently some hesitation about moving too quickly. For his part, Coach Haskins went after the best players, period. His record speaks for itself. At the beginning of the 1965-66 season, more than one observer noted the large number of black players on the Miner team and brought it to the attention of the school's president, Fitzpatrick—summoning the athletic director to discuss the issue. "It was going to reflect on me, no question about it," he reportedly said, "if we played all black boys." He told the athletic director to tell Coach Haskins that he couldn't play "more than three black boys" at the same time. Well, the coach objected, of course. "The way our boys line up now," he said, "my six best boys are black. If I leave two or three of them out because they're black, they'll know it. The white boys will know it. They all know who the best basketball players are, just as I do." That was the end of the issue. Coach Haskins was told to coach the team the way he saw fit.

●

As I said, Coach Haskins recruited me heavily during my senior year. I had visited the campus the maximum number of times permitted by the rules. Lloyd really wanted me to go to Tennessee State, and I thought El Paso was just too far away from Houston, even if it was still part of Texas. I appreciated Haskins' commitment to winning, though. Unlike the other coaches, who promised I would get the ball and would score the kind of points I was used to in high school, Coach Haskins told me I would have to be unselfish and play for the good of the team. It would mean I'd score less, but the team would win more, and that was what mattered. I liked that.

There was one strong reason for attending Texas Western over Tennessee State, and it really pulled at me. Jim "Bad News" Barnes had attended there and had set a slew of records, making a national name for himself. He'd shown me how you could shine on a team like Texas Western, and that Coach Haskins played a style of ball that allowed it.

Coach Haskins wrote that he told Barnes he could do for Texas Western what Elgin Baylor had done for Seattle; that is, turn it into a basketball powerhouse. That first year with Barnes, Texas Western went 19-7. In his senior year, the school went 25-3, and he averaged 29 points a game. He established a Field House record in one game, hitting 23 of 26 field goal attempts. He put Texas Western on the map and in so doing established more records than I can list. These include the most points in a game, at 51; the highest scoring average for a season, at 29.2; most free throws attempted in a season, at 295; the most made, at 210; the most rebounds in a single season, at 537; and, at 299, the most field goals in a season. These records were established his senior year.

Barnes also holds all-time school records in scoring average, at 24; highest field goal percentage, at .532; best rebound average, at 17.9; and the most rebounds at 965. He was an All-American, and in 1964, he won an Olympic Gold Medal. The NBA New York Knicks took him as the first pick in the first round, and he was selected as All-Rookie that first year.

I knew all the records at the time and told Coach Haskins I wanted to beat every one of them. Barnes was a hero to me, and I could think of no greater way to honor him than to break his records at the same school. It held a strong pull, but I also had my friends I wanted to help, and Tennessee State said it would take care of them. So,

I KNEW ALL THE RECORDS AT THE TIME AND I WANTED TO BEAT EVERY ONE OF THEM.

much as I wanted to go to Texas Western, I enrolled instead at Tennessee State.

Coach Haskins was working hard to assemble a fine team, recruiting where others didn't. He thought he should have won the NCAA championship with Barnes his senior year and was still determined to do it. He didn't have me, the dominant center he'd hoped for that next year. What he had were Willie (Iron Head) Worsley, Nevil (the Shadow) Shed, and Willie (Scoops) Cager who had all been recruited from New York City. Orsten (Little O) Artis and Harry (the Cricket) Flournoy both came from Gary, Indiana while Bobby Joe (Slop) Hill was from Detroit.

One of them, as I would be, was a transfer, one was a junior college dropout, still another averaged only three points a game. One player had to be dragged back to school after not returning from a semester break, and finally, Worsley was so short that he was routinely mistaken for the team's ball boy. In addition to the seven black players, there was one Hispanic and four white players.

Most of all Coach Haskins had Bobby Joe Hill, in my opinion the finest guard to ever play collegiate basketball. I'm still in awe of what that man could do with a ball.

Coach Haskins assembled these players in an unusual way, one that came back to cause him some unjustified grief. Cager, for example, dropped out of high school to help support his mother and brothers and sisters. A friend of Coach Haskins, Willie Brown, had seen Cager play, and also watched Nevil Shed when he'd attended North Carolina A&T. Coach Haskins trusted Brown and signed both players, sight unseen.

Coach Haskins also trusted Hilton White, who had been stationed at Fort Bliss and knew El Paso. He understood the opportunity Texas Western could give young black men and knew that they would be treated well in El Paso. He supervised a playground in New York City where he coached teams and saw a lot of players who were off the radar of the big schools.

Coach Haskins' deal with both men was that he'd do everything he could to see to it that any players they brought to him got a good college education out of their athletic scholarship. The academic record of his players speaks for itself.

What Coach Haskins assembled was a team of enormous strength and potential, assets that had to be harnessed. It was a team about which Coach Haskins often expressed exasperation. "It was a battle, every day," he said later. "It was a strange bunch, I tell you." I can only agree. That we were.

But before this team was put together, Texas Western had to play the 1964-65 season without "Bad News" Barnes, and it was a struggle, as was to be expected. Coach Haskins had really hoped I would step up to fill that hole in the team, but I didn't until the next year.

Attending all-black Tennessee State was a mistake, I quickly realized. They'd honored their deal for my friends and given them scholarships, making it possible for them to go to college, but the school really didn't play that much of a basketball schedule, something I should have paid closer attention to.

What nagged at me were all those records set by "Bad News" Barnes at Texas Western. Breaking them there had meant more to me than I realized. By the end of that first quarter, I knew I had to make a change. This just wasn't going to work. I dropped out of school, went home to Houston, and told Lloyd Wells what had happened. To stay sharp, I played on one of Lloyd's AAU teams. Lloyd, I have to mention, thought he was still a basketball player at age 40 and would put himself into some of the games with amusing results. But that was Lloyd.

I needed to be in college; I wasn't going anywhere playing AAU ball. I talked to him about what had happened in Tennessee State, and he understood. He was always on my side. As word spread that I was again available, I began receiving calls from coaches, one of them from Don Haskins to Lloyd Wells. Lloyd called back, and Coach Haskins said he'd still like to have me. He couldn't buy me a ticket, the rules didn't allow that, but if I arrived on campus, he'd give me a scholarship. Lloyd bought me the airplane ticket, and Assistant Coach Moe Iba picked me up at the airport. It was January, 1964.

Coach Haskins wrote later that he figured I was going to be a problem. I was big, I'd made demands while still a high school student, and I acted as if I had an attitude, but that was all show for the opponents. I worked hard, and I took care of myself. I never gave Coach Haskins any reason to ever regret taking me after I'd turned him down.

I had to red shirt the rest of that year, which meant I couldn't play on the varsity team, but I could work out with them, and I liked what I saw. I had a very good feeling about my decision to come to El Paso once I was there.

The white players on the team had been in previously integrated schools, so there were no race issues on the team. Even better, El Paso was a liberating experience. It seemed to me that Texas Western and El Paso were not only progressive, they were the future—they had to be. We black players were well treated in town, in part because we were stars, but also because the historical racial issues in sleepy El Paso had always been Anglo versus Hispanic. Blacks were always on the sidelines, a nice place to be.

Still, there was almost nowhere the team could hang out publicly, not for racial reasons so much as because we were so young, and El Paso didn't have that many choices anyway. The much larger and livelier Mexican city of Juarez lay just across the river, I rarely went there for recreation, though the rest of the team did. Juarez had long welcomed the servicemen, white and black, from nearby Fort Bliss, and the Texas Western basketball players fit right in. Or so I'm told.

Over the years, I've said many kind things about the people of El Paso. I meant, and mean, every word of them. I'm not alone. Nevil Shed had attended North Carolina A&T before transferring to Texas Western. In North Carolina, there were white and black drinking fountains, and when he bought a ticket to the movie, he paid full price for the privilege of going through a back entrance and sitting in a filthy balcony. None of that existed in El Paso. It was for him, for all of us, a breath of fresh air, a precursor of what *could* be, of what *would* be.

There are many similarities between Adolph Rupp and Don Haskins. They both coached in similar ways, they'd both gone to colleges where they had great success at an early age and had gone there straight from coaching high school. But in other ways they were very different. Coach Haskins was committed to building the best team he could. Coach Haskins went out and signed the best players he could find, regardless of race, taking them from city basketball courts, if necessary. Coach Haskins put on the court his five best players, regardless of race, and that meant they were usually black.

Attending Texas Western, though, was for me, for all the team, about more than playing basketball. We intended to get an education, to leave with a college degree. An athletic scholarship was the only way any of us could get one, so I didn't just play basketball. I majored in Communications and on Sunday night hosted a jazz program, the Soul Room, on the college FM station. With Dave Brubeck playing in the background, I would set up the next tune. I was known as Big D or Big Daddy D. Okay, I was a big man on campus. It was great.

The style of play I was taught there was new to me, though I'd always played center and been concerned with defense. Coach Haskins was *very* defense-oriented, and defense, frankly, is hard to play. It requires commitment and intelligence. It's much easier to dribble down the court, pass the ball, then take a shot. Much easier. Dropping back quickly, assuming a defensive posture, playing aggressive man-on-man, which is what we did, is demanding and difficult.

Before the start of that first season, something unusual took place, something I'd never experienced before. We were attending a dinner in a downtown hotel ballroom with some 500 boosters, the usual kind of thing you do before the season, a chance for the boosters to get close to you. We sat at a table up front and listened to the coach speak. Coach Haskins was apparently very pleased with us, which came as news to me. He said, "Listen, these guys are special. This is a special team."

That perked me up. I thought we were good, too, but I'd never heard a coach brag about a team *before* it produced and was more than a little surprised. I took it as a sign that we were as good as I thought we were.

> I TOOK IT AS A SIGN THAT WE WERE AS GOOD AS I THOUGHT WE WERE.

That we *were* good came as no surprise to me, because I'd always played on winning teams. My junior high school team was undefeated, and I'd been selected as the best player in the city. My senior year as a high school player, we only lost two games and won the state championship. Playing on the freshman team at Texas Western, we only lost one game and routinely beat the varsity in practice. I was used to winning and expected nothing less. I hadn't come to college to start losing.

Coach Haskins was also used to winning and intended to win it all. That required the best team he could assemble, one he worked hard. It also meant putting the best player in every position on the court all the time. If they happened to be black, so be it.

CHAPTER 6

TEAMMATES

We didn't know black or white.

TEXAS WESTERN'S WILLIE WORSLEY

EL PASO, TEXAS, IS about as far removed from my hometown of Houston as a small town in New England. The difference is just as great, even though they are in the same state.

El Paso is the site of the longest continuously occupied settlement in Texas. It was named by the Spanish for the place where the Rio Grande River, which marks the border between the United States and Mexico, cuts through the Franklin Mountains. Its identity has long been the result of its proximity to Juarez, Mexico, and to the nation of Mexico. It has a mild climate and a generally quiet way of life.

Because it is on the southern route for traveling from the East to California, El Paso has always been a stopping-off place. A military post that was located there in 1849 was eventually named Fort Bliss. The Buffalo Soldiers were stationed there and began the history of an African-American minority finding acceptance, or at least tolerance, in the town and across the border in Juarez.

In 1913, the Texas Legislature created the State School of Mines and Metallurgy in El Paso. Within a short time, an 18-acre campus was secured, and by 1918, the five main buildings were completed, to some controversy. The wife of the college dean had seen pictures in a *National Geographic* magazine of the isolated Himalayan country of Bhutan. The terrain seemed to her to resemble that of El Paso, and she urged her husband to have the new campus constructed to resemble Bhutan's so-called Castles in the Air. Painted a light gray or beige with a red band near the gently angled roof, they are distinctive and utterly out of place but over the years have been accepted.

In 1955, Texas Western was the state's first four-year college to integrate. The following year it integrated its athletic program, the first college in the southern United States to do so. Because the school did not play in the Deep South or even in East Texas, but played a schedule of mostly integrated schools to the north and west, black athletes in competition on the Texas Western court were unremarkable.

But in general, the school lacked distinction until 1960. It was then that the student body began the increase that would lead to it doubling in size over the next eight years, and the curriculum was broadened. The modest basketball program had enjoyed some success in 1941, when it won the Border Conference championship, but for the most part the team had losing seasons until the mid-fifties.

When it came to race relations, Texas Western was a Renaissance College. When the spotlight of public opinion was directed on it after we won the title, its example helped push open doors for thousands of deserving black athletes, enabling them to receive college scholarships and the education that went with them. Many successful minority men and women, whether they know it or not, have Texas Western to thank for the opportunity to obtain their college education.

For me personally, the environment of El Paso and Texas Western offered a tremendous opportunity, but it was a world apart from where most of us came, particularly the black players. Willie Worsley was from a very tough South Bronx area and had never been on an airplane before he flew to El Paso. He wanted to take the bus but agreed to fly when told the bus trip was two and a half days. He said he'd never been scared in his gang-infested neighborhood, but climbing aboard that airplane scared him to death. He found his aisle seat, then a white lady also flying to El Paso climbed over him to sit by the window. She soon struck up a conversation, and when she learned he'd never flown before, gave him her window seat so he'd have the view, then showed him how to fasten his seat belt. Cars didn't have them in those days, and he'd never seen one before. Later in the flight, when his ears were clogged, she gave him gum to chew to help clear them.

"This person," he said, "was treating me like her son. She didn't try to put her purse away. I thought, *If the people in El Paso are half as nice as this lady, I'll be comfortable.* And when I got there, they were."

A few years before I arrived at Texas Western, new college leadership made the decision that a winning athletic program could help energize the college and bring it much-needed attention. The fastest way to do that was to recruit often-overlooked black athletes to its athletic program. There was a great pool of quality high school black players not being tapped by other schools, and this represented a tremendous advantage to the obscure college. With this objective in mind, Don Haskins was selected as the new basketball coach.

A month after his hire, boosters helped pass a $30 million bond issue to build a new football stadium for the college. In 1963, the Sun Bowl was inaugurated to bring spectators to the stadium and tourists to the city. The former stadium, Kidd Field, had an average of 4,500 attendees. The new stadium was soon drawing 25,000 to the Sun Bowl. In the four-year period leading up to 1964, contributions to the Miner athletic department grew from just $25,000 to more than $125,000.

But the primary sport was basketball. Barnes was right. El Paso was a basketball town. In 1961, tiny Halliday Hall was abandoned for the new Memorial Gym with 4,600 seats. In 1963, the NCAA held tournaments there, while the NIT did in 1965, a first for both. These were significant events, precursors of a program that was coming of age.

I knew none of this when I enrolled in January, 1964. I had visited El Paso three times, as I recall, when Coach Haskins had been trying to recruit me. What I remembered about the small town was how quiet it was, with very little going on, especially when compared to Houston, and how friendly the people were. It was, I soon realized, an excellent environment for study and for playing basketball.

THESE WERE SIGNIFICANT EVENTS, PRECURSORS OF A PROGRAM THAT WAS COMING OF AGE.

My arrival set the campus buzzing with excitement, I've been told. Students tried to sneak into practices to watch me. It was an amazing experience and just a precursor of what was to come.

I've read that Juarez and its temptations were a constant concern to Coach Haskins, and I can understand that. He didn't want us getting into trouble. There were a lot of nightspots and dog racing. Though I wasn't a regular visitor to Juarez like some of the other players, I recall visiting the track once or twice.

I had a full athletic scholarship, which included room and board. Board meant eating in the student body cafeteria, at the well-stocked athletic table, where I ate all I wanted. Food, and hunger, were never a problem at Texas Western. I had a room in a student dormitory which housed about 200 other students. When I first arrived, my roommate was Bobby Joe Hill, whom I'd never met before. The hot music for young people at the time was rock and Bobby Joe loved it, but I was into jazz and I think after a few months it wore him out. Anyway, he moved out, and I got a room of my own, you know, big man on campus.

I think we were paid some cash as part of our scholarship, something like $12 a month, but none of this was about money for us. Anyway, the team boosters took good care of me. I don't mean they slipped me envelopes like I've heard happened at some schools, but in their places of business, well, you understand. I was given tickets to games by students and could sell them to boosters; they were generous in buying them. But in general, all I had was a bit of pocket money and that was that.

For me the best perk was the jet that the local mining company shuttled between El Paso and Houston three times a week. I could always get a seat and got to see my mother whenever I wanted. When you're that age and away from home, that means everything.

In the spring of 1964, I was red shirted. I was permitted to practice with the varsity team and also played ball in town with soldiers from Fort Bliss. Over that first summer, I worked for a steel company in Houston, the kind of job employers gave to young college athletes. As I recall, my job was to watch pipes go by on a conveyer belt.

I was working hard at getting better at basketball, and eating at the athletic table at college and with my mom at home, I was certainly getting bigger. After work and on weekends, I played pickup games in the park against some very fine athletes. I also played in a summer league with Carroll Dawson, Don Cheney, Phil Harris, Lucius Jackson, and Elvin Hayes, to name a few.

That fall, I returned to school, and we began playing ball at once. We all loved the game and loved to play. Officially, Coach Haskins couldn't be there. We'd gather at agreed times and play, but I'm pretty sure he had eyes on the court as we often received instructions on what to do, what to improve on.

Official practice began in October. That year I played on the freshman team. Some of the players on the championship team were with me there as well. We only lost one game and scrimmaged against the varsity team, beating them regularly. I also routinely trained and worked out with the varsity team. By the time 1965 arrived, I knew every player intimately and had played with, and against, them all. All of us had been imbued with Coach Haskins' system and knew it inside out. There were no surprises when preparations for what became the championship season began.

As I mentioned, Bobby Joe Hill was my first-year roommate. We became great friends. We saw each other regularly for the rest of his life, and we often talked about writing this book together. I wish we had. He died very unexpectedly in December, 2002 at the age of 59.

Bobby Joe was a happy man who always had a smile on his face and a friendly word. Five feet, ten inches tall and 170 pounds, he was from Highland Park in Detroit, where his father worked at the Dodge factory. Bobby Joe was All-City his senior year, averaging 23 points a game. He'd attended Burlington Junior College in Iowa out of high school and then dropped out. Coach Haskins, I understand, had seen his outstanding play at a National Junior College tournament his freshman year, then later learned he wasn't attending school and recruited him after he had sat out a year and gained 50 pounds.

Coach Haskins had said that Bobby Joe was as good out front as Nate Archibald was in college. He was quick and was a great defensive player who would fit in exactly with what Coach Haskins wanted from his team. Fitzpatrick wrote that Coach Haskins said he was shocked to see how much weight Bobby Joe had gained in his time away from college ball. Here his future quick guard, was now weighing 230 pounds. Bobby Joe set out to prove he still had it and promptly ran rings around the team's best players in practice, even carrying that excess weight. The rigorous training schedule soon had him trimmed down.

Bobby Joe played two years for Texas Western, his sophomore year and then our championship year when he was a junior. He was a great ball handler, maybe the best ever, an excellent shot and rebounder—a natural. Everyone on the team was his best friend.

From my experience and in my opinion, Bobby Joe was the finest guard to play college ball that year, and had he played in the NBA, he would be a household name today. I don't expect to ever fully recover from his tragic death.

We had two great rebounding guards.

The other starting guard was the very quiet Orsten Artis. At six feet, one inch and 175 pounds, he was also a great rebounder. Bobby Joe had the reputation for being our best outside rebounder because he was all over the court, but years later I checked the statistics and found that Orsten had out rebounded him by 2 percentage points. When I told him, he was quite surprised.

THE WAY WE PLAYED OFFENSE, WHOEVER WAS OPEN TOOK IT. IT MADE US VERY DIFFICULT TO DEFEND AGAINST.

Orsten was a star at Groebel High School in Gary, Indiana. He'd been highly sought after by a number of schools including UCLA and Oklahoma, but not for his fine rebounding. He was a great and natural shooter with an outstanding open jump shot from outside. He was perhaps the only player on the team Coach

Haskins never objected to taking a shot. If we were going to take an outside shot, we preferred it be Orsten, but you couldn't always know from where the shot would come. The way we played offense, whoever was open took it. It made us very difficult to defend against. He and Harry Flournoy came to Texas Western as freshmen. They had each been spotted on a scouting trip by Coach Haskins, who'd already heard about them from a former Oklahoma A&M player.

Flournoy was six feet, five inches tall, weighed 200 pounds and played forward. He was also a quiet guy. He'd been highly recruited as a great rebounder. He didn't score all that much, and when he did it was from layups or this sneaky little hook shot he had. A bit beefier than Shed, he was a classic defensive player. The story goes that he was walking home from high school one day when he noticed a white man following him slowly in his car. The driver got out, and Coach Haskins introduced himself. He then asked if he could meet Flournoy's mom. At their home, he told her about the program at Texas Western and what he had in mind for her son. She served him coffee and a slice of her homemade pie, which as the story goes, he declared to be the finest he'd ever eaten. Flournoy signed shortly thereafter.

Nevil Shed was the other starting forward. He'd played in the Bronx at Morris High School and learned about Texas Western from Hilton White. He was six feet eight inches, 185 pounds, which meant he was skinny. He was the only player on the team who could guard anyone—center, guard, or forward. He was an extrovert, always talking, very outgoing. I'd always assumed he played center in high school and college ball, but he was a perfect forward who played well facing the basket. He had an astounding open jump shot from 15 to 20 feet out that played devastation on the opposition.

He originally attended North Carolina A&T before coming to Texas Western. The story goes that he was suspended for violating a curfew and left school that first year. Coach Haskins heard about it, called him on the telephone, and offered him a scholarship to go to El Paso.

Then there was Willie Cager. He was six feet, five inches tall and weighed 170 pounds. From New York City, he had not graduated from high school until he was recruited by Coach Haskins. He'd played ball in the New York recreation leagues and learned how Texas Western treated black players. He went to El Paso on his own and went to work at a service station, sleeping in back of it while he attended school and over the summer obtained his GED so he could be admitted to college and take the scholarship. He was outgoing, quite talkative, and obviously motivated. He played both forward and guard, depending on what the substitution called for when he came in the game. He was a great ball handler with a full set of flashy moves and could take the ball to the hoop against anyone.

Fitzpatrick wrote that Coach Haskins told him that Willie had a heart murmur. "We would play him about four minutes at a time and that would make him furious," Coach Haskins told him. "His mother wanted him to play, but we didn't like putting him on the floor too much. Cager could score. He was not a great shooter, but he'd figure out a way to get it in the basket. He was a great sixth man. Sometimes we'd put him in there and say, 'Willie, make something happen.'" And he did.

Willie was a classic sixth man before the position was identified as such. If a game was on the line at the end, Cager was always on the court, because he was a decent rebounder and a great scorer. Frankly, I don't even want to think about what our season would have been without him.

Then there was Willie Worsley, of the airplane. He was short at five feet, six inches and weighed 165 pounds. He was an only child, raised in a rough South Bronx neighborhood. He had played playground ball and was, to put it politely, tough. You didn't want to mess with him. He led DeWitt Clinton High School to the city basketball championship his senior year and was a high school All-American. Worsley had been named Most Valuable Player of the championship game, which had been played in front of 18,000 fans at Madison Square Garden. He was a great outside shooter, a decent rebounder, and a really outstanding defensive player, despite frequent size differences with those he guarded. He was quiet, with that certain New York attitude, the same thing Shed had. Obviously, he played guard.

Worsley knew Willie Cager, Nevil Shed, and another player at Texas Western, so going to little El Paso was not that big a deal for him. Worsley, Cager, and Shed had all played in New York City's inner-city competition where Cager was a legend on the city courts with his acrobatic play.

What those who remember Worsley's play recall was his ability to dunk the ball. That's right, five feet, six inches tall, and he could stuff the ball through the basket. The feat is even more impressive when you realize that his small hands didn't allow him to palm the ball, which is a tremendous advantage when you dunk, so he had to jump even higher to pull it off. I was impressed every time I saw him do it. At every game, during warm-up, Worsley dunked the ball several times. The first time he took to the basket, you could hear the sucking of air, then the "Aaahhhhh" from the crowd.

In fact, everyone on the regularly playing team, except for Orsten and Hill, could dunk. It was our most powerful offensive weapon.

There is more to a team than the starters and the regular players. These guys are typically called bench warmers, a term I consider to be insulting. They serve a vital function because you have to have quality players to play against in practice, but there's a lot more to it than that. On our championship team, the difference between the regular players and nearly all of those who saw much less playing time was very, very little, and given more time, who's to say they would not have been just as good as the others. You need these guys; you seriously need them. Without them we would have never made it to the national championship. One observant reporter described our bench talent as "bottomless."

Willie Worsley said about the non-starters, "It's kind of funny, but things worked out the opposite of how they did everywhere else then. But whatever has been said, and I hope I can say this correctly, we could never have been where we were if it wasn't for the five other players on the team. They were our competition in practice, our buddies

WE COULD NEVER HAVE BEEN WHERE WE WERE IF IT WASN'T FOR THE FIVE OTHER PLAYERS ON THE TEAM.

off the floor. In all the years we were together and all the years since, we never talked about race. We never had an argument. We had some battles, just like two babies playing in the same pen. But we didn't know black or white. Ask any of the black players and they'll never say anything bad about our white teammates. They wanted to get playing time, but that was normal. We did everything together. They played cards with us. They joked with us. We had water fights with each other."

And there's Lewis Baudoin, who told Fitzpatrick, "There's complete acknowledgment from the regulars that without the contributions of the second five in practice, it would never have happened."

Absolutely.

So we had Lewis Baudoin, who was from New Mexico. He was red headed, six feet, seven inches tall, 200 pounds and a great outside shooter. He was one of those who would have been a starter elsewhere and really deserved to play a lot more than he did. He only played in 16 games that season, but he's the one who made me work hard in practice. He was very outgoing, sometimes to a fault, saying things we all thought but didn't utter. He was funny and bright, perhaps a bit closer to Bobby Joe than were the others.

There was six feet, four inch tall, 220 pound Jerry Armstrong from Missouri. He was, as you'll see, vital to our advancing to play in the title game that season. He was tough, good at defense and rebounding, and a fine outside shooter.

There was also David Palacio, the only Hispanic on the team. He was six feet, two inches tall, 180 pounds and was from El Paso. He was a good outside shooter who could drive to the hoop. He was, for obvious reasons, a crowd favorite whenever he took the court at home. At home, when we were well up, the crowd often started a chant to get David into the game.

There were two more on the team who almost didn't play during games. One was Togo Railey, six feet tall, 175, also from El Paso. He was a decent shooter and a great teammate. I've always figured he was someone Coach Haskins wanted to give one of the 12 scholarships to. The other player was Dick Myers. He was six feet, four inches, 185 pounds and from Kansas. He was a good outside shooter and a decent rebounder.

It was hard for all of us to be away from home, but I suppose toughest for the guys from New York City. Fitzpatrick quotes Coach Iba saying, "El Paso is a long way from anywhere.... The thing about El Paso was that very few of them got home very often. When they came to school they were at school from the end of one summer to the beginning of the next. It was hard but, hey, these kids knew hard. And for a lot of them this was the best they ever had. They got to go to school. They had a good place to sleep, three meals a day, an opportunity to get an education. They were glad to be there."

Yes, we were.

That was the team. All of us knew one another well and had played against and with each other before that championship season. It was my first time on the varsity team, and I was technically a sophomore, but I'd been playing with these guys for 18 months before official practice started that fall. In fact, the only new players to the varsity squad were myself, Worsley, Cager, and David Palacio, so the team was already a cohesive unit.

It was, in my humble opinion, a very good team that only lacked a center to be great.

David Lattin holds the ESPY Award for the movie *Glory Road* "Best Sports Movie of the Year 2006", starring Schin Kerr who played the role of David Big Daddy "D" Lattin.

James Gartner, Director of the movie *Glory Road,* and Schin Kerr, who starred as David Latti in the blockbuster movie, with David Big Daddy "D" Lattin

SLAM DUNK
TO GLORY

Worthing Is State Champ

PRAIRIE VIEW — (Sp) — Worthing of Houston won the 4-A Negro high school basketball championship here Saturday, defeating Madison of Dallas, 62-56 in overtime.

IN SNAPPING undefeated Madison's 24-game winning streak, Worthing was led by David Latin, voted the tournament's most valuable player, and Fred Callaway in overtime after the score was tied, 54-54 at the end of regulation time.

The Colts reached the finals by defeating Tyler, 81-63. Madison advanced with an 81-76 victory over Beaumont Charlton-Pollard.

LATIN SCORED 59 points in two games and was joined on the 4-A all-tournament team by Henry and, William Gaines of Madison and Bubba Smith of Pollard.

Lubbock defeated Fidelity Manor of Houston, 63-52 in the 2-A finals while Como of Fort Worth defeated Carthage in the 3-A finals, 57-56.

DAVID LATTIN

Latin Heads West Team

BY JIMMY BLAIR

Basketball will add to its stature as the truly all-American sport next week.

Fort Worth Terrell raised it to one peak in the 1962-63 season and the first annual East-West All-Star Classic will hoist it to another on July 1 in the Texas Southern University Gym.

The cream of the basketball teams in the Gulf Coast area goes to the firing line with Collin Briggs and Doc Evans heading the West unit and Robert Campbell leading the East team.

One quick glance at the team roester for the both units would make any coach feel well and honored with some many talented players for one season.

With David Latin heading the West team - well it could be real rough for the Easterners. Latin one of the most sought after schoolboy players in the state made not only the All-State and All-District but was listed on the All - American Schoolboy

Latin will be caked up by some tough lads - Robert Cerbron, Melvin Singletary and Thedore Frazier plus other lads.

As for the East team - it definite will have speed built around Nathaniel Loftis, Henry Smith, Gus Allen, Harry Gunner and Llyod Barnes.

Without a doubt Campbell will go for the zone defense against the supposedly shotting of the West team which has Latin, Cebron and Durham going for the outside.

Nothing is being taken for granted but one thing is sure - basketball will be at its best when the two team take to the hardwood floor.

In basketball, however, one constellation marely moves on to make way for another. Who'll be the game's brightest star?

It could be any one of players but mo perts feel te a well-balanced will pay off.

ERIC GOLDMAN & HAROLD HUN

EAST ALL-STAR TEAM ROSTER

Player - School	Pos.	Ht.	Wt.
Harry Gunner, Lincoln (PA)	C	6-5	190
Otis Booker, Kirbyville	F	6-4	175
Lloyd Barnes, Hebert (Bmt.)	F	6-3	175
Otis Booker, Kirbyville	C	6-8	218
R. Roseman, Kirbyville	G	6-2	182
Henry Smith, Central (Galveston)	G	6-0	155
Nathaniel Loftis, Central (Galv')	F	6-0	165
Gus Allen, Central (Galveston)	G	6-0	170

WEST ALL-STAR TEAM ROSTER

Player - School	Pos.	Ht.	Wt.
David Latin, Hous. Worthing	C	6-6	190
Rovert Cebron, Hous. Yates	G	6-1	170
Melvin Singletary, Hous. Yates	F	6-4	180
Leotis Durham, Hous. Yates	G	6-2	165
Theodore Frazier, Hous. BTW	F	6-3	185
Robert Lilly, Hous. Kashmere	F	6-2	175
Robert Jackson, Hous. Worthing	G	6-2	165
Leroy Smith, Wheatley (SA)	C	6-7	190
Ernest Smith, Hous. Kashmere	F-C	6-4	170
Joe Guzman (Regan, Hous)	F-G	6-0	170

ATTIN

one of the most sought after schoolboy players in the state

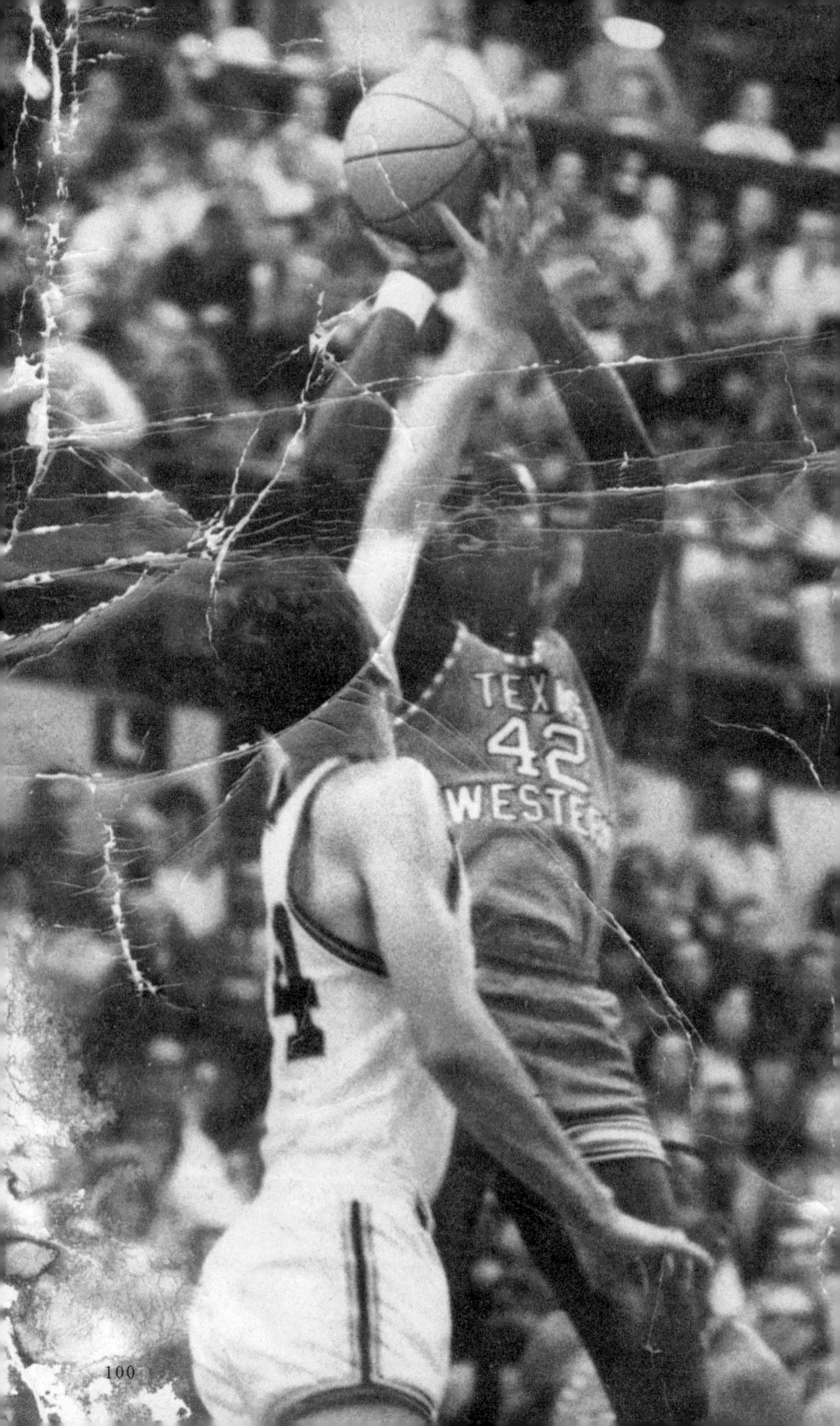
TEX
42
WESTE

YATES CAGERS FLUNK LATTIN TEST

Miners Get Driver
TWC Wins With Ease At Tempe

By BOB INGRAM

Texas Western had passed a difficult driver's test today. The Miners, it's apparent now, can play on any highway and basketball court in the country.

They faced their first big road exam of the season last night at Tempe, against Arizona State.

They passed it with a high grade of efficiency, beating the Sun Devils, 84-67.

THE VICTORY was the 13th straight of the season for the Miners. It was their first win in six tries at Tempe. It was a Don Haskins' first as far as a victory by his team in the Arizona city is concerned and it it was the worst licking a TWC team ever handed a fivesome coached by Ned Wulk.

The triumph, accomplished much easier than expected, should insure Texas Western's sixth place national rating for next week.

THE MINERS flew home today and had an afternoon workout scheduled for their game tomorrow night against the West Texas State Buffaloes at the TWC field house. Next Tuesday the Miners meet New Mexico State at El Paso.

The Miners in whipping the Arizona Staters beat a so-called Tempe jinx, the ASU home court advantage and the 21-day layoff they had for craming and exam taking.

As it turned out, they didn't look a bit rusty. Their near-easy victory can, among other things, be ascribed to these facts: Poise, balanced shooting and defensive play, their very good depth and a tremendous game from the Miners' strongboy, David Lattin. He played his most outstanding game of the season, shotwise and boardwise.

TIGHT IN SOME games this season, the Miners were a relaxed group at the start and were casually-like slipping their shots through the netting instead of banging the ball hard against the hoop.

As has been pointed out all season, TWC's strong bench is a big asset to the club. That might have been the big difference in last night's game. TWC was in foul trouble early. Four of the players had three personals at halftime. They were taken out and benched for awhile, as is customary in such situations. Then finally, two of them, Harry Flournoy and David Lattin, fouled out and Nevil Shed went out with a shoulder injury with almost nine minutes in the game left.

THE MINER replacements did not hurt Texas Western's drive. Arizona State did not have the manpower to spell its tiring and fouled out players with effectiveness.

In the opening minutes of sparring the game was tied 7-7. ASU never came as close to TWC again during the game. Twice in the first half, the Miners had 13-point leads. They were ahead 40-33 at halftime.

ASU poised a stiff threat at the opening of the second half. They cut the TWC lead to three and five points on different occasions.

THE PENDULUM began swinging definitely for the Miners, however, with 13:45 left. That was when Orsten Artis stole the ball and raced down the floor for a layup. The Miners edged ahead slowly and surely. Their margin reached 23 points with around five minutes of play left.

In field goaling, TWC had a percentage of 48 as compared with ASU's 39. The Miners hit 74 per cent from the free throw line

THE DEVILS, surprisingly, led TWC in rebounds 52 to 40.

Dennis Hamilton, 6-8 inside man of Arizona, led the scoring parade with 24 points. Two players on the TWC team, Lattin and Hill, tied him in the number of field goals, eight. Artis, however, was the Miners' high man with 19, 11 of which he made from the foul line. Lattin and Hill each had 18.

Lattin had some fine jump and stuff shots for the Miners and was a good man for them on the boards. He was a key factor in the win. The 6-7 Houston soph came through with an outstanding job.

TWC (84)	FG	FT	RB	PF	Tot.
Hill	8-16	2-4	3	2	18
Artis	4-6	11-12	4	3	19
Armstrong	0-1	1-2	2	1	1
Shed	4-8	0-0	6	5	8
Flournoy	2-5	0-1	6	5	4
Lattin	8-14	2-2	6	5	18
Caper	2-6	6-7	6	2	10
Palacio	0-1	0-0	1	2	0
Daudoin	1-2	0-0	0	0	2
Worsley	0-1	4-7	2	1	4
Myers	0-0	0-0	1	0	0
TOTALS	29-60	36-55	24		84

x—Texas Western had 6 team rebounds.

Ariz. St.	FG	FT	RB	PF	Tot.
Lewis	5-12	4-4	4	5	14
Bailey	1-2	3-3	1	1	5
Myers	1-5	0-0	2	4	2
Hamilton	8-18	8-9	12	3	24
Lange	4-13	0-0	8	1	8
Coppola	0-0	0-0	0	0	0
Lindner	0-2	0-0	1	0	0
Tuff	0-2	0-0	0	1	0
Magin	1-2	2-4	2	4	4
Whitehead	2-8	0-0	4	4	4
Walker	1-2	0-0	0	1	2
TOTALS	25-64	17-30	x52	26	67

x—Arizona State had 9 team rebounds.
Score at half: Texas Western 40, Arizona State 33.
Turnovers—Texas Western 13, Arizona State 17.
Officials: Don Miranda and Henry Murdock.

ASU Surprises Miners Without Zone—

Shooting, Defense Draw Haskins' Praise

The game with Arizona State at Tempe was proof again to Don Haskins that the Miners may be the best shooting team the school has had since he's been here.

"And I figure that our defense, especially in the first half, destroyed Arizona State," Haskins said.

"Our defense was so good that it kept Arizona State from playing their game." (A lightning fast break type of game.)"

Miners' Lattin 'All Greek' To 'Pokes

(Continued From Page 1)

helped the Miners to a 35-31 halftime pad.

Texas Western never again trailed although three straight baskets by reserve Cliff Nelson enabled Wyoming to pull even, 47-47, at 13 minutes.

Lattin immediately put his mates back in control. He rebounded in a short banker, and poured in two power layins to build the gap to 55-47. The 'Pokes could never come closer than the final margin.

The Miners, by missing four foul shots in five attempts, left an opening for Wyoming to creep through in the final two minutes. Texas Western was leading, 68-61, when Nelson hit four points and Eberle holed a banker.

This shaved Western's lead to 68-65. Willie Worsley's one-pointer built it back to four, but at 22 seconds Eberle found Hall with a floor-length pass for an easy layup.

It was the end of the scoring, however, as the Miners ran out the clock.

Lattin, who converted 11 of 20 field goal attempts, is a slick operator around the basket and is cleverly graceful despite his 240-pound bulk. Believe, too, that no one moves him around in the maneuvering for position.

His primary offensive weapon is a delay jumper, either off the glass or straight in the hole. Lattin will hook from in close or if needed, pepper from long range. His strength at pushing the ball through a forest of defenders is difficult to combat, and he was operating here with a deep charley horse.

Miner Coach Don Haskins wasn't happy with his defense, but added, "With all the injuries and other things which happened to us this year, we could have lost more games. And shooting has been our biggest problem all along."

The 1966 NCAA champs finished 22-6 to Wyoming's 15-14. In this consolation test, Wyoming the boar shooting committe Texas W

BIG D

'Big D' Is On The Air

By RILEY HALL

If you're not hitting the boo
tonight or Saturday at 7 p.
tune in on Dave Latin, ali
"Big D," on KVOF FM on yo
radio dial.

That's right—the well know
6-7 high point star for the TWC
Burros basketball team has
program over the air, featuring
your favorite jazz selections.

Among the recording artists in
Dave's collection are the incom-
parable Nancy Wilson, Jimmy
Smith, Arthur Franklin and re-
nowned Dave Brubeck.

"I worked at Station KCOH in
my home town of Houston last
summer," says Dave "and gained
a lot of experience in broadcasting."

The big center for the Frosh
has an excellent personal jazz
album collection which he sup-
plements for his program "with
collections from the boys at the
dorm."

AFTER THE GAME IN THE LOCKER ROOM

NOW THERE ARE FOUR

In the battle for the national basketball championship only Duke, Kentucky, Utah and Texas Western survive. If last week's pattern is confirmed, the final round at College Park will be the hottest in years by FRANK DEFORD

It was 8 o'clock Sunday morning in Lubbock, Texas, the morning after Texas Western upset Kansas in double overtime to win the Midwest Regional, and Don Haskins, the winning coach, was propped up in bed in Room 410 of the Eldorado Motel reading the Lubbock *Sunday Avalanche-Journal.* He had eaten a hamburger after the game, it had not agreed with him and he had not slept very well. The fact that his team had won two overtime games on successive nights, Haskins allowed, might also have been a contributing factor to the insomnia. But mostly, Haskins maintained, it was just the bad burger.

It is safe to assume, time zones aside, that at about this hour, in Durham, N.C., Iowa City, Iowa and Los Angeles, three other coaches were also stirring uneasily. It had been a mighty long season, starting with the players running cross-country in the fall, and now here it was March 13 and in all the land there were only three coaches besides Don Haskins, reading the Sunday paper in the Eldorado Motel, who had teams that could still win the championship.

There was Vic Bubas, home with his wife and three girls in Durham, N.C. His Duke team had just beaten St. Joseph's and Syracuse over in Raleigh to reach the NCAA finals for the third time in four years. Bubas is from Gary, Ind., a redheaded Yankee who has built a basketball dynasty at Duke and who has himself become the father image of organization and planning in his sport.

There was Adolph Rupp in Iowa City, ready to return to Lexington, Ky., where he is truly The Baron, the most famous basketball coach in history, the only man ever to coach four national champions. Kentucky had beaten Dayton and Michigan, and now, at age 64, The Baron only needed two more victories for his fifth title.

There was Jack Gardner, The Fox, in Los Angeles. His Utah team had just whipped Pacific and Oregon State, despite the fact that Gardner had lost his first-string center with a broken leg. Utah is the only school ever to win the NCAA, the NIT and the AAU back when the last-named tournament meant something. Gardner himself has won 551 games.

It is almost always the topflight coaches like these who get their teams to the finals. And it is certain that on this Sunday morning as they awoke, their first thoughts were of the games coming up on Friday night in College Park, Md. They eagerly anticipated the return of their scouts from the other regionals, laden with the precious raw material of X's and O's. The season had gone too

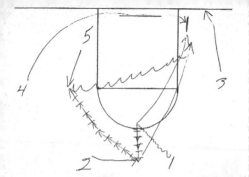

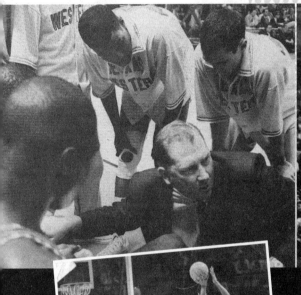

Big Man Hurt NYU

NOTHING BUT NET

NO. 42 DAVID LATTIN
UTEP MEMORY MAKER

David Lattin with Willie Worley and Bobby Joe Hill

1966-67 Center
6-7, 240

Home: Houston, Texas
MVP 1966 NCAA Midwst
  Regionals

Nickname: Big Daddy D

Drafted: 1st Round NBA, 1967
San Francisco
Played: NBA Warriors, Suns,
ABA Pittsburgh and Harlem
Globetrotters

Facts About David Lattin

☐ Averaged 19.3 points in NCAA play
☐ Averaged 10.6 rebounds in NCAA play
☐ Played only 2 years of collegiate basketball before opting for NBA career
☐ All-time UTEP scoring leader in NCAA play
☐ Closed out his UTEP career with his best performance, scoring 34 points and 13 boards against Wyoming in NCAA tournament
☐ His UTEP coaah, Don Haskins, is still amazed, Lattin, at 6-7, could dominate a game
☐ Scored double figures in 44 of 56 career games at UTEP
☐ Had double figure rebounding in 27 games
☐ Scored in double figures in 16 straight games as junior and 14 as sophomore
☐ Named MVP in Midwest Regional (NCAA) with 44 points, 25 rebounds against the likes of Cincinnati and Kansas

Big Daddy D and the NCAA

Yrs.	Opponent	Fg/Fga	Pct.	Ft/Fta	Pct.	Reb.	Pts
1966	Oklahoma City	8/15	.533	4/5	.800	15	20
1966	Cincinnati	10/15	.666	9/10	.900	8	29
1966	Kansas	7/16	.437	1/2	.500	17	15
1966	Utah	5/7	.714	1/1	1,000	4	11
1966	Kentucky	5/10	.500	6/6	1,000	9	16
1967	Seattle	4/6	.666	9/13	.692	14	17
1967	Pacific	6/13	.461	1/1	1,000	5	13
1967	Wyoming	11/20	.550	12/13	.843	13	34
	Totals	**56/120**	**.549**	**43/51**	**.843**	**85**	**155**

David Lattin's UTEP Totals

Yrs.	Gms	Fg/Fga	Pct.	Ft/Fta	Pct.	Reb.	Pts.	Avg.
1966	29	148/299	.494	111/158	.703	248	407	14.0
1967	27	143/302	.473	123/176	.699	273	409	15.1
Totals	**56**	**291/601**	**.484**	**234/334**	**.700**	**521**	**816**	**14.5**

1965-1966
TEAM STATS

	G	FG	Pct.	FT	Pct.	Reb	Avg.	PF-D
Bobby Joe Hill	28	161-392	.411	97-159	.610	85	3.0	73-2
David Lattin	29	148-299	.494	111-158	.703	248	8.6	114-11
Orsten Artis	28	141-300	.470	72-83	.863	98	3.5	53-0
Nevil Shed	29	116-235	.494	74-98	.755	229	7.9	5.2
Harry Flournoy	29	96-192	.500	48-74	.649	309	10.7	4
Willie Worsley	29	81-201	.403	69-96	.719	66	2.3	5
Willie Cager	27	55-134	.410	68-100	.680	108	4	
Louis Baudoin	16	17-44	.386	1-5	.200	20	1.0	
Jerry Armstrong	24	12-43	.279	21-24	.875	33	1.4	
David Palacio	15	6-24	.250	2-5	.400	8	0.5	
Dick Myers	14	4-12	.333	4-8	5.00	9	0.6	9-0
Togo Railey	4	0-0	.000	1-2	.500	0	0.0	0-0
Team Rebounds						206	7.1	
*TWC Totals	29	864-1899	.446	568-812	.699	1430	49.3	581-19
Opponents	29	647-1614	.401	523-739	.709	1050	36.2	601-36

*TWC totals includes two players not listed.

'Twas Defense That I

Western Texas NCAA Champion

NCAA FINAL FOUR

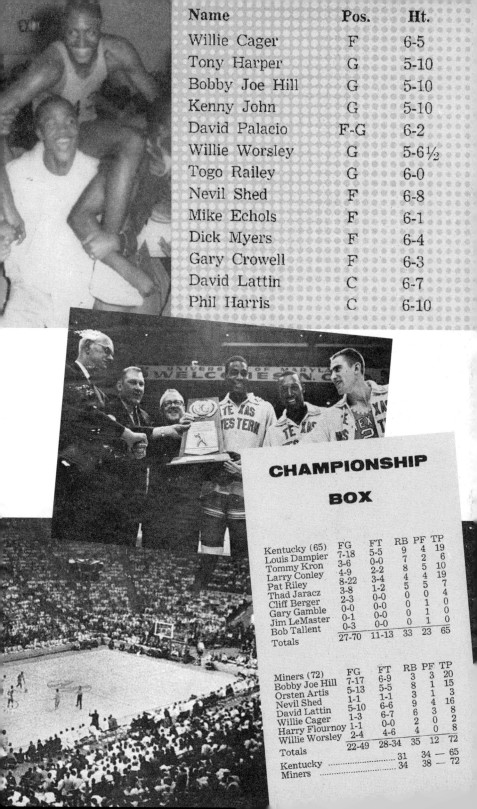

Name	Pos.	Ht.
Willie Cager	F	6-5
Tony Harper	G	5-10
Bobby Joe Hill	G	5-10
Kenny John	G	5-10
David Palacio	F-G	6-2
Willie Worsley	G	5-6½
Togo Railey	G	6-0
Nevil Shed	F	6-8
Mike Echols	F	6-1
Dick Myers	F	6-4
Gary Crowell	F	6-3
David Lattin	C	6-7
Phil Harris	C	6-10

CHAMPIONSHIP BOX

Kentucky (65)	FG	FT	RB	PF	TP
Louis Dampier	7-18	5-5	9	4	19
Tommy Kron	3-6	0-0	7	2	6
Larry Conley	4-9	2-2	8	5	10
Pat Riley	8-22	3-4	4	4	19
Thad Jaracz	3-8	1-2	5	5	7
Cliff Berger	2-3	0-0	0	1	4
Gary Gamble	0-0	0-0	0	1	0
Jim LeMaster	0-1	0-0	0	1	0
Bob Tallent	0-3	0-0	0		0
Totals	27-70	11-13	33	23	65

Miners (72)	FG	FT	RB	PF	TP
Bobby Joe Hill	7-17	6-9	3	3	20
Orsten Artis	5-13	5-5	8	1	15
Nevil Shed	1-1	1-1	3	1	3
David Lattin	5-10	6-6	9	4	16
Willie Cager	1-3	6-7	6	3	8
Harry Flournoy	1-1	0-0	2	0	2
Willie Worsley	2-4	4-6	4	0	8
Totals	22-49	28-34	35	12	72

Kentucky	31	34	— 65
Miners	34	38	— 72

CHAPTER 7

THE SYSTEM

We were always practicing.

TEXAS WESTERN'S LOUIS BAUDOIN

ALL OF US UNDERSTOOD the value of Coach Haskins' system and how it would lead to victories. Nobody fought it or practiced with it less than aggressively. We were at school to win, not to go through the motions. The year before, the Miners had gone 16-9 and had been invited to the National Invitation Tournament, where they were eliminated in their first game. That was a record on which we wanted to improve dramatically.

One tremendous advantage we had was that every one of us loved to play ball. We didn't look to basketball for our identity or to make us special. We just loved the game; you almost had to run us off the court. During the off season, we played ball every day. During the season we held our own unofficial scrimmages on Sundays. Even before official practices began, we held formal games against ourselves. We even had a couple of local teams come in to scrimmage against us.

Coach Haskins had his own routine, as do all coaches. Practice was held six days a week and on school days began promptly at three o'clock, just after classes. We practiced for exactly three hours. Practice was played at game intensity, which is one area where those who didn't play as much during games were so important. They couldn't be chumps the rest of us walked over. They had to be good and play like they meant it. It made all the difference when we played for real.

Coach Haskins was merciless with us, but all of us were on the same page in that regard. He wanted us to be the best and we wanted to be the best. He was, frankly, a brilliant defensive coach, and the defense he devised was tailor-made for the team he recruited. For it to work, his plan required great players, and that we had. No great coach ever won without great athletes, but Coach Haskins was, without question, the greatest coach I ever had.

I read once that the ancient Spartan warriors welcomed war, because it was easier than their peacetime training. In our case, the practices were tougher than the games. We never hit the floor in practice with smiles on our faces. It always reminded me of being on a job, a job I loved, but still a job.

Bobby Joe once said, "We used to run there to get to the front of the line, because the water got warm in a hurry.... Man, we used to pray for those games to get here. The practices were killing us."

This new style of play was tough on lots of the players who were used to shooting the ball whenever they wanted. Fitzpatrick tells one story that was probably true for a lot of the players on the team. During an early practice with the team, Nevil Shed broke free on a fast break and ran towards the basket shouting for the ball, which never came. He was ignored because that wasn't the way the team played.

"Coming from New York City, it was a fast pace," he told Fitzpatrick. "You know, run and gun, run and gun. Not a nice neat passing game. [Now it was] bounce, bounce... I remember Coach Haskins saying, 'Son, in this program we pass the ball. You're not back there in one of them city-slicker places. We pass the ball.'" And pass we did.

The story goes that when he noticed Nevil shying away from me, he pulled Nevil from practice and took him to his dorm room. There he threatened him with a ticket home, dragged out his suitcase and started pitching Nevil's clothes into it, all the while ranting at him. Nevil kept trying to take his clothes back, telling Coach Haskins he didn't want to go home.

OUR STYLE OF PLAY WAS ANYTHING BUT THE FLASHY STEREOTYPICAL GAME OF TODAY.

That night we scrimmaged again, and Coach Haskins told Nevil to take it to me. He went up to get a rebound from me and ended up getting his nose broken. I didn't mean to do it. It was just the way we played. But after that he was a different, and better, player.

Our style of play was anything but the flashy stereotypical game of today. We played smart, we played disciplined, and, frankly, it was a pretty boring style to watch. Our emphasis on defense and rebounding is the kind of formula that leads to championship success in college basketball and the NBA far more often than does the flashy style you see on television game highlights. The team with the highest scoring average rarely, if ever, wins titles. The champion is usually the team with the best defensive statistics.

Much has been written about Coach Haskins' manner towards us; how he yelled a lot, complained about how lazy we were, how sarcastic he was towards us. Playing the kind of defense he wanted was demanding, and we did have a tendency to turn it off and on as we thought necessary. If the other team wasn't being effective, we would ease up. We knew we could always turn it on.

I personally always got along with the coach, and because I practiced so hard, I was not one of the players he yelled at. Though I loved to practice, I knew some of the others hated it. From my perspective, practice was how I got better. I loved that it was all business, with no fooling around.

Orsten later told Fitzpatrick, "What he was trying to instill we just couldn't see. We were there just for fun, you know. We thought practicing was for people who couldn't play."

During practice, we would play defense for two hours and forty-five minutes. Really. Then the coach would give us 15 minutes to play some offense. He knew we could score. It was his belief that in the heat of a game, the offense of teams tends to be about even. The real difference was in defense, hence the emphasis he put on it.

This was the exact opposite of how I practiced in high school and how we played. But Coach Haskins had explained when he was recruiting me that I'd have to give up some of my points for the good of the team. He told me how he intended to win, and it made sense to me.

Though we spent most of our time in practice on defense, during games we worked to keep the ball; that is, to stay on the offense. The idea was that as long as we held the ball, the other team couldn't score. It tended to take most teams out of their game plan. It also meant that the other team played a lot of defense, usually zone.

Now, a zone defense is easier than man-to-man, and that's why most colleges use it. Its one great defect is that it concedes the outside shot with the hope it will miss. But it also has another weakness: it is really boring to play. We found that Coach Haskins was right. If you forced a team to keep playing zone the entire game, eventually they begin to make mistakes, not from fatigue so much but from the sheer repetition of the moves. It just gets old, they get very frustrated, and it's difficult to keep it up for an entire game. Eventually, they give you an opening.

Ours was an enormously talented team that could have succeeded by playing in several different ways. What Coach Haskins taught us worked, so there's no criticizing it, but the truth is that we were a Porsche that had to drive at 55 miles per hour most of the time. We did that because we believed in ourselves and Coach Haskins. But I'm of the opinion that had this been a run-and-gun system, we still would have won the NCAA title. We were that good.

There was no shot clock in those days, so we came down the court and passed the ball at our own pace. We only broke into a fast break if we fell into the situation and couldn't suppress our instincts. Despite the system in which we were coached, we were a very quick team. Our speed caught more than one opponent by surprise, especially, since we moved around at such a plodding pace so much of the game.

Typically, once we got the ball into their end of the court, we did a lot of passing, as we were under no time pressure. Coach Haskins violently objected to anyone shooting the ball after just a single pass. The idea was to keep the ball in motion, to keep the ball out of their hands, to eat up time, to search for the genuinely open shot rather than to force one. The best shot was inside to me. The next best shot was an open jumper from outside or a drive on the basket.

As I said, we had no preferred shooter on offense, so a defending team couldn't focus on one or two players and shut us down. On offense, our guards worked the ball back and forth, looking for an opening. If either of the forwards was free, the ball went to him. If I was free, the ball came to me.

My most feared weapon was the dunk, and I don't use the word "feared" lightly. I saw fear often enough when I made my move to the basket. The dunk was not new that season but was still not commonly seen in play and was strongly identified with black players from inner cities.

Coach Haskins encouraged me to dunk or "to flush it," as he put it. He prohibited behind-the-back dribbles and passes, but realized that our ability to dunk intimidated opponents. I loved to dunk, had dunked as often as I could in high school, and he urged me to dunk as soon into a game as possible, to set the mood, so to speak.

Once I had the ball, I rose to and above the rim, then jammed the ball through the basket with one or both hands. Once I had position, it was impossible to stop. It was a take-no-prisoners statement of domination. Though a dunk scored the same two points as a layup, the effect was completely different. A dunk was "in your face." It was fierce and intimidating.

Coach Haskins had us play man-to-man on defense. This is much more demanding than the zone defense, and it requires very skilled and bright players to make it work. As demanding as it is physically, it is also very mental and requires great mental toughness to maintain throughout an entire game. One advantage is that it never leaves a player open to take an uncontested shot. It meant we stole the ball more often than other teams. When it's working, it is beautiful to watch.

The system was rigid as could be, and woe to the player who switched. Lewis Baudoin once said, "We played man-to-man and never switched. If you switched, you came out of the game. I remember one time a kid came out of the game and was sent to the locker room to change his clothes because he switched on defense. It was very serious.... But that discipline was exactly what we needed because we were eighteen, nineteen-year-old kids who all came from a variety of cultures, neighborhoods, and families. We had to have one unifying thing to keep us going and that was it. It was simple and straightforward and there were very few rules. You were on time and you didn't miss class."

It also meant that everything the other team wanted to do came only with effort. By guarding each player aggressively, they were challenged just dribbling the ball. When they attempted a pass, the defender sought to deflect the ball or knock it away. Even the player for whom the pass was intended found himself having to fight to catch the ball. Nothing a team prepared in practice came easily to them against us. We challenged everything. It denied a team the back and forth of passes that set up shots. It took them out of their own game.

We had another tremendous advantage over the teams we played, because we were coached to do something most teams didn't. To this day, I'm surprised so few teams do it, and it was the reason we were the number one defensive team in the nation our championship year. Texas Western had been ranked as one of the top five defensive teams four years in a row before that. That year we gave up a meager 62 points a game.

On defense, the guards maneuvered inside the foul line for the deep rebound rather than break for the other end of the court. This meant that if I didn't get the rebound or either of the two forwards, if the ball bounced out deeper than we could handle, they were there to get it, or at least to contest for it. All of our guards were great rebounders.

There is something about us that is never mentioned, and I've always believed it contributed greatly to our success. Three of our five starters were left-handed. This is a real advantage in most any sport, and it certainly is in basketball. The majority of players are right-handed, so when you defend against them you get used to the hand they favor, the side they tend to drive towards. The lefty does it the opposite way, and it is very hard to defend against.

You can remind yourself the player is left-handed, that the usual rules don't apply, but basketball is played at such a speed that you respond from instinct. It gives the lefties that little bit of advantage. Our left-handed players were Bobby Joe, Shed, and Flournoy. Lewis Baudoin was also left-handed. In all, four of the twelve players were left-handed. It was simply awkward to play against them, because most players don't run into lefties that often, certainly not those who played ball at that level.

THIS WAS MY TEAM, THESE WERE MY GUYS.

There's been a lot of talk that we were different in the championship game because of our race. If we were different in a way that made us distinct from the other teams, it was in our number of left-handed players, not the color of our skin.

I was not immune to the psychology of winning. In high school, I had adopted a certain attitude around and on the court and found that it made my job a bit easier once the game started. If the guy covering you was, well, afraid, he'd tend to shy away at crucial moments, so my body language and manner during warm up and during the game was to intimidate. I brought cockiness, coolness, a certain take you down attitude to the team. I've always believed that was my greatest impact.

There's something more. This was my team, these were my guys. My job was to protect it and each player. They knew that, and I believe it gave them a certain extra measure of freedom. No one was going to stomp on them, not a second time at least.

As part of my program to dominate, I dunked the ball 100 times in practice. It really helped my timing. During warm-up before a game I would dunk seven or eight times, then jam one down the basket as early in the game as possible, just to make a point. Yeah, we were a great defensive team, but we had our offensive skills as well.

I'm told fans several rows back jumped out of their seats when I dunked the ball. This was in the days before the spring-loaded rim, and the backboard would rattle, as if it were about to shake apart. One reporter described me landing "with a menacing thud, and [a] Sonny Liston scowl..." Good. I hope the players saw it like that, too.

The way we played on defense was intended to deny the other team the outside lanes, so that they would be forced to come up the middle. It was set up so that the offside guard would come over to help, then the forward from the offside would come in to help, to clog it up in the middle; then they had to face me.

Moving to the basket up the middle was to enter "Dangerous Country" where, frankly, I lurked eagerly. Because we were a relatively small team, my role as center was about dominating the boards and establishing a brutal inside game the opposition dared not challenge. I was used to that, and that was one reason why Coach Haskins wanted me.

As Nevil Shed later put it, "First you had to get by Bobby Joe and Orsten out front. Then you got to Flo and me, the Shadow. After that, you met the Man [Lattin]. If anyone drove the lane on us, we would knock his lights out. For the brave ones, it used to get cloudy in there real fast."

You need a great guard to win, and we had that in Bobby Joe, but you have to have a great inside player as well, and that's where I came in. I was the enforcer. If any player tried to take advantage of one of the "little" guys on the Miners, I would have a talk with him and make my point. In one game that season, Worsley went in for a layup and was catapulted into the stands. I was quick to make my presence known and there were no more problems after that.

But for all my physical strength and dominating presence, I played the game with the finesse of a light and quick player. I'd learned I had to. With my short cropped hair and the nickname of "Big Daddy D," referees paid me special attention and I couldn't help us win from the bench.

We had other advantages as a team. As I said, the five starters and the two primary substitutes were all fast. We considered any pass we failed to deflect or a dribble we neglected to obstruct to be a personal affront. No one was supposed to look good against us. Bobby Joe and Orsten met the opposing team at half-court and from that point on made their presence on our end pure agony. They pestered them every second, constantly looking for a steal. Worsley was just as bad, or good from our point of view. From inside, I knew it was working as it should when I would see the other team practically running in circles trying to get open to make a pass or take a shot. It was almost comical sometimes.

Every one of us on that team brought specific skills, talents, and experiences to that season. Individually, we were all-stars. "We were like the strings of a guitar. Each one was different, but we sounded pretty good together," Willie Worsley said about us. I couldn't agree with him more, and even if Bobby Joe was singled out as our spiritual leader and I was "The Man," we were just two players on an enormously talented and hardworking team.

As I say, we were a very physical team with an attitude of toughness about us. I contributed to that and encouraged it in others. Coach Haskins knew our demeanor gave us an advantage even before the first tip-off. Some reporters took it all seriously and in writing about us wrote as if we were a gang of thugs spoiling for a fight. One called us "This renegade band from the badlands" as we arrived for the Final Four. What we were was a very talented, self-confident team looking to get an edge.

Nevil Shed once told a reporter, "People called us misfits and ruffians. That's not true. We had poise and we were disciplined; without discipline and poise you could not play for Coach Haskins."

Our key assistant coach was Moe Iba, and I've always believed his impact on the team was as important in making us a success as was that of Coach Haskins. Moe was a great team guy. His father had won many games as a head coach and had taught Coach Haskins when he was a player.

Now, Coach Haskins is easily the best free throw shooter I've ever seen. Every player on that team improved his free throw shooting under him. To make a point he once shot 200 free throws in a row, enough to make us beg him to stop.

Coach Iba was one of the greatest outside shooters I've ever seen. Shooting from 40 feet, he once made 75 of 80. He was amazing. They liked to play, showing off, demonstrating they knew how to do this, too.

People wonder sometimes why players listen to coaches. Maybe that tells you just one of the reasons. Coach Haskins was such a defense guru that you wouldn't think he could shoot like that, but he unmistakably could.

OFF THE COURT, WE SPENT A LOT OF TIME TOGETHER, AND THE PLAYERS HELD EACH OTHER IN HIGH REGARD.

Moe scouted the other teams for us and learned what they were doing. He always saw the good teams play, then he would give us a 10 or 15 minute chalk talk, show what they did, who the players were and what they could do "This is the game they are trying to play, these are their stars, their strengths and weaknesses."

Coach Haskins would then set up those conditions in practice. See what I'm getting at about the players with limited time during the games? They had a demanding job and really had to throw themselves into it. Because they were so good, it was a very effective technique.

Off the court, we spent a lot of time together, and the players held each other in high regard. There was no animosity of any kind between anyone. We all wanted the same things. My teammates used to play a lot of cards. It was friendship, pure friendship. I don't remember a single instance of race being an issue or a problem among us." And so it was.

The real issue on the team, as on all competitive teams, was playing time. Willie Worsley told Fitzpatrick, "I know it's hard for people to believe now, but we were just kids. Just kids who played basketball. 'Black' didn't enter our minds. We were concerned about getting playing time and about getting through practice because that man was working us like dogs. That was my priority. Playing time. I'm a ballplayer. I was used to playing thirty-two minutes in high school. I always had the ball in my hands. I was the main man. Now I was surrounded by eight other main men."

Though practice was always scheduled for after classes, if you had to take a lab, Coach Haskins was good about letting you go. He understood that we were also students and that, for many of us, an athletic scholarship was our ticket to a college education.

People sometimes suggest that when I talk about the warmth of the people of El Paso, I'm exaggerating, so let me tell you about part of it. In the dormitory, there were always study halls and study groups. Everyone was helpful. It was a very supportive environment for me and for the others on the team. The teachers were good about make-up classes and tests, on top of it. I couldn't have asked for more.

That's what the campus was like for me and for the others. The hardest part of school and the season was the traveling. You had to take your homework with you on the road and, I'm telling you, those were tough study conditions.

CHAPTER 8

THE MAGIC SEASON

[Lattin] had license to slaughter.

TEXAS WESTERN'S LOUIS BAUDOIN

NO ONE WAS EXPECTING Texas Western to win anything, and we started the season unranked. This proved a tremendous advantage to us. For the early part of the season, then later in the play-offs, no one saw us coming. I don't believe we were ever scouted. When we arrived at the Final Four in Maryland, the sportswriters had never seen us play. All they'd heard were rumors, and some of the teams in our schedule were not exactly powerhouses. That made it easy to overlook our victories against very tough teams.

We thought we were good as our first regular season game approached, but we had all played enough basketball to know you have to prove it on the court. We didn't talk about how good we were among ourselves, and when we took the court, there wasn't a smile to be seen. I had confidence in my team-mates and went into the first game with high expectations.

Our schedule that year was pretty much the same as the one Texas Western had been playing in recent years. There were a number of good teams on it, enough that if we won we would get noticed. The season started in November and ended in February unless you advanced to postseason play. We played twenty-three regular season games that championship season. About half were played at home. On average we played two or three times a week, though there were weeks, as I remember, when we only played one game. We played every day of the week, but Sunday.

For away games we typically flew out the morning of the game, played, spent the night, then either flew back home or on to the next game if we had two in a row on the road. People talk a lot about home-court advantage, but I never found that to be true if you were really good. The basket is the same height everywhere, the court is the same size. There might be, and sometimes was, a bit of difference in refereeing, but otherwise it was all the same. When you are a good team and play to your level, you take the hometown crowd out of the game. I could never hear the crowd, because I was so focused on what I had to do. In fact, I preferred road games.

I had been taught by all my coaches that you don't think about the games down the road. You focus just on the game coming up, and I have to say we were very good about that. We would arrive well before game time. We dressed, stretched, and had warm-up. Coach Haskins had little to say at that point; it had all been said in the days leading up to that game.

Ten minutes before we were to take the court, he would have us all lie down and stretch out, then he killed the lights. This was a time for concentration and reflection. We were to visualize what we had to do, how we were going to play the game. You might even say it was sort of a mind-relaxing exercise.

Once we took to the court, Coach Haskins called a huddle, but only to remind us of the points he had made during practice and of what to look out for, and to mention again key players and the team's strengths. Then it was up to us. That was often what he said: "Now it's up to you."

Frank Fitzpatrick in his book *And the Walls Came Tumbling Down* writes that Coach Haskins would eye our opponent in the opening minutes of the game, then call out the number of the player we were to take it to on offense. It wasn't like that at all, and I'm not sure why he had that impression. What we did was identify their best ball handler in those first moments, then give him the middle to drive. That first foul was meant to make a statement about the game, to let them know they were in for it. He would drive for the basket, and along the way one of us lowered the boom.

As Baudoin put it, "We would waste the first foul. He always had a history of big bruisers in the middle, so maybe the first time they came down on offense, we would pick up some dancing guard and turn him into the middle. Someone like Lattin would take his head off. The rest of the team and their bench would see it, and that would set the tone."

I don't recall any heads rolling on the floor, but he got it right, except it wasn't always me. I knew the referees were gunning for me and I had to be careful, especially in those opening minutes, otherwise I would be out of the game in no time.

But the point was to be intimidating, to get them out of the game they wanted to play, to have them concerned for their safety on the court. It's a tremendous advantage and one that served us very well that season. Fitzpatrick got that part right—

teams shot terribly against us, hitting only 40 percent of their shots. We made 45 percent of ours and out rebounded opponents more than twelve a game. It made all the difference. It made us champions.

We won our first games with relative ease, and I was feeling good about our chances after the regular season. These early games had been against Eastern New Mexico, East Texas State, Pan American, Weber State, Fresno State (twice), South Dakota, and Nevada, the last two in the Mississippi Cage Classic at Rock Island, Illinois. The only one of those to give us any trouble was the first game against Fresno State.

To this point in the season, our opponents had been less than stellar, not teams to really test us or draw national attention, quite understandably. Our first significant victory was during the championship game of the Sun Carnival Basketball Tournament, held at Texas Western over the Christmas holiday. Three other teams were invited to participate, one of them being Iowa, who ranked fourth nationally in one poll and sixth in another. For that reason, the Iowa Hawkeyes were the heavy favorite to win the tournament.

I KNEW IT WOULD BE A GREAT GAME AND WAS GLAD TO HAVE IT AT HOME WHERE THE FANS WOULD APPRECIATE WHAT WE COULD DO.

Even though we stomped on the floundering Loyola team in the first round, the Iowa coach must have been pretty cocky about his team's prospects, because he foolishly said at a press conference before our game that he didn't think his team would be challenged until the first game of the NCAA tournament at the end of the season. We all read that and smiled.

I knew it would be a great game and was glad to have it at home where the fans would appreciate what we could do. We knew we were good but had no idea how truly good we were. Because of their ranking and what their coach had said, we were out to dominate them from tip-off. We turned the defense on from the first moment and took no prisoners that the first half, smothering them right off. They didn't even know what was going on.

With something like three minutes left in the first half, the score was 23-6 and we were leading. The game was over for all practical purposes. I guess the Hawkeye players had read the same newspaper we had. They managed to score with just four free throws and a ball Shed accidentally tipped in for them, sort of a gift from Texas Western. Their center was a big guy, six feet nine inches as I recall, but he gave me no trouble. If they weren't embarrassed during halftime, they should have been.

From those opening minutes there was never any doubt who would win. We coasted the second half and ended up winning. The score was 86-68, and the game wasn't even that close. We had shown them, and I left the game knowing we were just as good as I'd thought we were. I don't recall that the Iowa coach had anything much to say after the game, at least not compared to what he had said before.

We were listed in the top ten for the first time since "Bad News" Barnes had played at Texas Western, and the fans were delirious. Coach Haskins later wrote that he was surprised we had handled such a talented team with such ease and that he considered that game to be the real start of our march to the NCAA championship.

Following this victory we had a three-week layoff to cram for and take tests. We then traveled to Tempe, Arizona, to play a very good, fast-break-oriented Arizona State University team. I heard that week that Coach Haskins had never defeated ASU in Tempe in five previous efforts and wanted to very badly. They were an excellent team with a couple of good black players, but there was never any doubt in my mind we would have a good game and beat them.

We played loose, and we played well. They made the mistake of playing us man-to-man. Our guards stole the ball repeatedly in the first half, and our defense forced ASU into many errors. The result was that we took them out of their game completely. We led by 23 points with five minutes left in the game. We shot 48 percent from the field to their 39 percent.

One reporter covering the game wrote, "Their near-easy victory can, among other things, be ascribed to these facts: poise, balanced shooting and defensive play, their very good depth and a tremendous game from the Miner's strongboy, David Lattin. He played his most outstanding game of the season, shotwise and boardwise."

That was a clipping to mail to mom, who was still raving about Elvin Hayes. I scored 18 points and had 6 rebounds, but our high scorer was Orsten Artis with 19 points. I was tied with Bobby Joe, though I only played twenty-eight minutes due to foul trouble. On top of that, Orsten held the Sun Devils top scorer to 14 points, seven under his average. My rebounds were the same as those of Flournoy and Cager.

Our easy victory there, 84-67, raised more than a few eyebrows. We established that we could not only beat a good team, as we had with Iowa, we could also beat a good team on their home court. What stands out for me about that game was the ASU coach saying afterwards that our team was for real and was going to do very well as the season progressed. This was our thirteenth win without a loss, and we moved into sixth place in the national rankings.

After we beat ASU so easily, a close friend of Coach Haskins told him that he thought we could go all the way. We were playing so well, though, that he didn't mention that to us. That is the moment, he later wrote, when the thought of winning the NCAA title first occurred to him.

Now, Coach Haskins has always complained that we were too cocky and too lazy. He says we drove him crazy, that we had some games that never should have come so close.

Well, to some extent I can understand his position. That might be how it looked to him. But we were not lazy. By this time we knew we could beat anyone. We knew our defense was so good that there was no team in the country we couldn't shut down at will. I guess it did make us a bit cocky, if that's what you want to call a strong degree of self-confidence. We were tested a few times that year when we found that we really couldn't just turn that wonderful defense on at will and shut a team down, but we never lost our belief that we were going to win any game we played.

I would point out that we had two All-Americans on the team that year—me and Bobby Joe—most didn't have any. You don't make All-American by being lazy. No other team in the country, not even Kentucky, won as many games as we did. Our record and performance spoke for us. No team could have had the Miner's record and won it all being lazy, period!

As our unbeaten record continued to grow, there was greater and greater excitement on the Texas Western campus and in the city of El Paso. No basketball team there had ever done so well. I'm pretty certain that our fans were thinking national championship before the thought ever entered our minds.

We nearly blew the perfect season to date though against our seventeenth opponent, the University of Arizona, when playing them at home. We were now ranked fourth in the nation, and the University of Kentucky with an 18-0 record was the only other undefeated team in major college rankings.

Arizona kept the pressure on us the entire game, never allowing us to establish our usual lead. Though Arizona was behind most of the night, they were always too close. Twice we managed a seven point lead and twice they closed the gap. We were ahead by just four points at halftime, and then Arizona roared back in the second half. Over a six-minute period, the lead changed hands *nine* times. Deciding enough was enough we hustled, Nevil put us ahead for good with a layup, and we won the game 81-72.

Our next major game was against our big rival, the University of New Mexico Lobos in Albuquerque. Coach Haskins has called it one of the greatest games he ever witnessed. What I recall most about it was the poor officiating. The downside of shaving your hair tight, scowling a lot on the court, and taking no prisoners when you move to dunk the ball is that you get a bit of a reputation. Because of that, when you arrive for a game, the referees already know your name, and that's not good.

I would have to guess at motives to account for what happened, and I won't do that. Fans like to think the referees are against the visiting team and in favor of the home team. I guess that can happen, but I didn't see it. I think it's more to do with showing you who's in charge. I think when you arrive with a reputation, like the one I had developed, the new referees may think that other refs have been too easy on you, maybe let you get away with breaking the rules, and they aren't going to let that happen. Sometimes officials just make mistakes. For some reason, it is easier for the referees to make them against the visiting team, because they get the approval of the dominating home crowd, which is understandable—we all want approval.

What I know is that I went into that game determined not to get into foul trouble. I didn't want to give those guys with the whistles any excuse. My recollection is that I got called for fouls that never happened right out of the gate.

Mel Daniels was their great center, and I couldn't even touch him. I couldn't even *breathe* on him. I couldn't so much as jockey under the basket, because they would call a foul on me. The referees simply didn't allow me to play at all, and I went on to foul out of that game in the first half. That's one of the reasons we were down 19 points at half-time. They had me out of there so fast I couldn't believe it. For the second half, I sat on the bench trying to figure out what to do differently next time, because I knew this would come up again.

With today's fast-paced games and shot clock, 19 points may not seem like very much, but the way the game was played then, with its much slower pace, it was a formidable, usually insurmountable an obstacle. As I've said, Coach Haskins had a system. We had been drilled in it, had practiced in it, and had used it to play successfully, but for whatever reason it wasn't working that night. So coach turned loose the reins, and Bobby Joe and Orsten got to play their game. They changed the landscape of that game quickly by simply doing what they really do best: press, steal the ball, run and gun.

We ate that team up in the second half, forcing the game into overtime where we won 76-64. There are times when you have to recognize that what you usually do isn't working and change the plan. Coach was smart, just like us, and we all wanted to win. That was our eighteenth victory in a row with no losses.

This was the one team Coach Haskins did not want to face in the postseason; they were very good, though I feel we were the better team. Fortunately for us, he has written, Utah beat them for the Western Athletic Conference title and advanced to the play offs. Utah made it into the Final Four where we faced them. Personally, I've always figured we would have defeated UNM, if we'd played them again, especially away from their home court.

Race was not an overt issue for me while playing during the season, but racism was very much on the radar during the 60's. If it hadn't been, I would have stayed at home in Houston, and attended my college of choice, the University of Houston, but race was not a large part of playing basketball during Texas Western's championship season, since we didn't play schools in the Deep South. We played out West where there was a much more tolerant atmosphere. I never heard a racial slur that entire year, but then I always tuned everything out on the court. If something was said, I never heard it.

For me it was about giving my best effort in every game. It was all about playing ball and winning games. We were just concentrating on winning every game, one after the other. As I recall, every team we faced, except for Brigham Young University, had at least one African-American player. Pan American, which we played twice, had as many blacks as we did, but otherwise we had the most black players on a team.

But race was a continuing issue for Coach Haskins. Fitzpatrick writes that a coach from a major Texas college had warned him that black players "don't have the capability to think when the pressure is on." Never mind the poise with which we played, the intelligence our style demanded, that absolute control we exercised over our defense and offense. It was assumed because our skin was dark; we were not intelligent.

We were lucky when it came to injuries. Looking back over the season, I noted that Bobby Joe missed one game, probably from an ankle injury. I recall no one with a nagging injury. But if there was a secret to our success, it was the quality of our bench. There simply wasn't a significant drop in talent, if a starter didn't play because of injury or fouls.

On a personal note, my mother never saw me play that season. There wasn't that much basketball on television at the time, and until I went off to play college ball, she never had much of an interest in it. As I did better and better, people would ask her how I was, shake her hand, and give her a warm smile, so she knew something was up.

That year Elvin Hayes was playing at the University of Houston, and because it was the local team, it was on television a lot. I would call to tell her about my latest game. "Mom, we won! We won!" I would say, and she would respond by saying that was very nice but, "Big E," as she called Elvin, "got 35 points, blocked 20 shots, got 12 rebounds, and the Cougars won!" She would be very excited about Elvin Hayes, although I knew she was very interested in my success on and off the court. All I could do was shake my head.

The Miners remained undefeated leading up to our last game. We were ranked number two, just behind the only other undefeated team in the nation— Kentucky. For all the similarity of our records, and the fact that neither team was very tall, we could not have been more different. Kentucky ran and passed like crazy, relying on the fast break to free one of their skilled shooters, usually Pat Riley or Louie Dampier, to sink an outside jump shot; this at a time when there was no three-point shot.

> WE WERE FIGHTING OUR WAY INTO BASKETBALL RESPECTABILITY, PLAYING FOR A COLLEGE NO ONE HAD EVER HEARD OF, AND WE KNEW IT.

On top of that, Kentucky was a basketball dynasty, and its players were the white royalty of college basketball. Adolph Rupp had appeared on the cover of *Sports Illustrated* that season, and the Wildcat starters had been on the cover of *Time* magazine, sporting the matching college blazers they wore when on the road. We were fighting our way into basketball respectability, playing for a college no one had ever heard of, and we knew it.

The media coverage about us as we wrapped up a near-perfect season was predictably disparaging. One magazine identified Texas Western as being "just a few rattlesnake lengths from the Rio Grande" river and compared some of the buildings to "the Alamo." The school possessed "a distinctive Southwestern flavor, like a pot of refried beans." Coach Haskins was mocked for "hunting varmints in his free time."

Our last regular season game was against Seattle, a team we had beaten easily earlier that year. We already knew that we had advanced to the postseason and, for the first time that year, we were looking past the pending game. We had beaten these guys and expected no trouble with them. We were focused on Oklahoma City, our first postseason opponent.

We were also watching the television in the lead-up to the game to see what happened to Kentucky, the only other undefeated college team. We'd followed them most of the year as we rose in the polls. Once we were number two, we were just waiting for them to trip up. Well, we learned that Kentucky had stumbled and lost their final game. We were elated. Our win against Seattle that night would mean we would enter the NCAA postseason play ranked number one. This was heady stuff given the lowly position from which we had begun.

So instead of knuckling under, we took that game for granted and ended up losing by two points. I personally missed three of my early foul shots, not at all like me, and reasoned we would have won if I'd only made them. I vowed that would not happen again. In fact, I did not miss a single foul shot the entire postseason.

I don't recall what Coach Haskins had to say to us after that miserable performance. I just know we deserved it. He later wrote that Bobby Joe and others kept trying to take the ball to the basket when it was clear the referees weren't going to call the fouls our way. I suppose. Memories of his college game at Oklahoma A&M against Kansas must have come home to him, but it was a good lesson to us. We weren't invincible. Even a team like Seattle could beat us if the breaks went their way.

Thirty-two teams advanced to the NCAA tournament that year. All season we had made a point never to look beyond the next game, except the one time against Seattle, and I took that to heart. For that reason, there was no talk about winning the championship or how far we would advance in the tournament. To win it all, we had to defeat five outstanding teams in a row.

What was about to happen was not generally recognized at the time, in part because other mixed-race teams had won NCAA championships in 1956, 1962, and 1963. But none of them had done it with five black starters or an all-black team on the court for the duration of the game. It was, in fact, a positive advance in race relations that the game took place at all.

Just four years earlier, the SEC champion, Mississippi State, had refused to participate in the NCAA tournament because the school would not play integrated teams, even though black players were excelling in the NBA, and many played superior ball on integrated college teams.

Kentucky wasn't the only segregated team, but it was likely the most famous. As one commentator later said, "You've got

Kentucky...standing out there as this major corporation with its doors firmly closed to minorities." The Southeastern Conference, Atlantic Coast Conference, and Southwest Conference, college basketball powerhouses, were all segregated.

For us, it was a lot simpler and had nothing to do with race. We were out to prove we were the best team in the country, and the humiliating loss in the last game of our regular season only hardened us. We were out to make history for ourselves and for the town and college that had been so good to us. It did not occur to any of us that we would play in a game destined to go down in American history as one of the greatest victories both in college sports and racial equality.

CHAPTER 9

GETTING THERE

The mood on the club going

into the tournament was anger.

TEXAS WESTERN'S LOUIS BAUDOIN

WE ATTENDED VICTORY PARTIES after every win, all season. Our last game was our only defeat, and we were flying to Wichita, Kansas, the next morning. As independents, we were required to win an extra game to enter the regular NCAA play offs and were next scheduled to play in the Midwest Regionals against a very tough Oklahoma City team. So, it was quite natural that Coach Haskins imposed a curfew on us for the first time. Primarily, I'm sure, was to make sure we got rest for the next night's game. Given our age and self-confidence, it was only natural that we ignored him.

Bobby Joe Hill, of course, had some friends in Seattle, and there was a party planned for us at a private home. We stayed in our rooms until bed check at curfew, then dressed and went, all except for Nevil Shed. He left, but then immediately returned for something he forgot and was in his room when Coach Haskins sent Coach Iba to conduct a second bed check of our rooms at the hotel where we were staying. Nevil heard the check going on and promptly jumped into bed, clothes and all, pulling the covers up to his chin to hide the fact that he was planning to leave for the party. He'd had a problem with curfew at his previous college, and I'm sure he didn't want to go down that road again.

The rest of us wandered back at three or four o'clock in the morning. Coach Haskins was furious. As one of the offenders, I was told I wouldn't be starting the game the next night, nor would Bobby Joe. Throughout the flight, Coach Haskins sent Coach Iba repeatedly through the plane to keep us from sleeping. This made absolutely no sense in terms of winning the next game. To win it all we had to win the next game in a few hours, and here was the coach refusing to let us sleep. Well, Bobby Joe slept anyway. Nothing was going to wake him up.

Lloyd, my mentor from Houston, met us changing planes in Chicago. On the second leg of the flight, he talked to Coach Haskins nonstop and asked him why he was cutting off his nose to spite his face, or words to that effect. Lloyd said, "Are you serious? You may never get here again. You've got the best team in the country, and you're going to kill your chances by punishing these guys for staying out past curfew. You aren't going to start Dave, you aren't going to start Bobby—are you losing your mind? You can't do that at this level. It doesn't make sense." And so it went for most of the long flight.

I credit Lloyd's persuasiveness, but there might have been more to what happened. Coach Haskins in his book, *Haskins,* tells about earlier setting a rule that any player late for a pre-game meal would be kicked off the team. Wouldn't you know it, his star showed up late and with a good excuse, but Coach Haskins felt trapped by his own words and cut the player. A good friend chastised him repeatedly over the incident, telling him such actions did no good, not for the team, not for the player. You save such punishment for truly serious infractions. Between experience and Lloyd, plus having been eliminated early previously, Coach Haskins relented—a little.

One reporter described us as stepping off the airplane with "poker faces" and said we were "an unemotional bunch." Right. I think we were dog-tired. Not much later, Coach Haskins held a take-no-prisoners practice and ran us into the ground, after which we slept like babies.

Oklahoma City was staying at the same hotel we were. One of the guards, a Native American, spotted Bobby Joe in the lobby, got in his face, and called him a little chump. Bobby Joe took the insult to heart and couldn't wait to get on the court. But when game time came, Coach Haskins started me and made Bobby Joe sit on the bench. The longer Bobby Joe sat down, the more worked up he became.

Oklahoma City was a high-scoring team. One of their stars was a six feet, nine inch, 260 pound forward, James "Weasel" Ware, who played very aggressively and typically garnered more than 20 rebounds a game. He was the nation's leading collegiate rebounder. Coach Haskins warned us not to fall behind this team, because it would be agony to catch up.

The other team came storming out after tip-off, and we reeled under the onslaught. For seven long minutes we struggled with this excellent team as Bobby Joe, infuriated, chafed on the sidelines watched us fall gradually behind. When we were down 23-18, Coach Haskins called a time out. He decided that was enough and called "Mr. Hill will you please enter the game!" Willie Cager went in at the same time.

Those two had Oklahoma City out of its game plan within seconds, and Bobby Joe promptly went on a mission, scoring 17 points in about six or seven minutes. He was later described as "a sleight-of-hand and sleight-of-foot man on the court." Sort of like a magician, I guess. He stole the ball twice that game while I even managed to pick off a steal. We were leading by halftime and went on to win 89-74. Bobby Joe had 24 points. Oklahoma City shot 44 percent and was out-rebounded 55-32.

As for Ware, well, he didn't do all that much that night. I had 20 points, 15 rebounds, and shut the man down. I ate him up, limiting Ware to 11 rebounds. The assistant coach at the UH later told me that "I'd skinned Ware." He would play really well when I was out of the game, and then he would pull into a shell when I came back in. What was interesting was that the NBA scouts in attendance were there to see him, not me. I showed up and did what I always did, protect, rebound, defend, score, and dominate.

When I read the comments of Oklahoma City coach Abe Lemmons the next day, I was pretty proud. He said, "Without Lattin, Texas Western is just a good team." Maybe, but without Bobby Joe we were just a good team, and without...well, you get the point.

The reporter went on to describe me in that game as "King of the Mountain" in my domination of Ware. One wrote that I "...nearly tore the basket down with a series of stuffed shots while beating James Ware, the nation's leading rebounder, into submission." He went on to say that I "...crammed the ball down the nets and literally down the throats of the Oklahomans." It was a team effort, but it's still nice to read things like that about yourself.

The comment elicited some playful press. A reporter went to Tay Baker of Cincinnati and asked what he thought of the merits of me over Bobby Joe. Baker had scouted the game and said that Bobby Joe was our standout player. So the reporter went to another coach, this time Jimmy Viramontes of West Texas, who settled the dispute. He said we needed both of us to win, that a bad night for either of us would be "ruinous" for the team.

Abe Lemons had more to say about Texas Western. "The Miners aren't good to watch, but they are clearly No. 1. I wouldn't play them next season if I had twenty home dates open. The Miners make you look bad. They won't let you do what you want to do when you get the ball. They aren't flashy like Duke or Kentucky—just tough."

Coach Haskins has written that our final loss turned out to be a good thing for the team, since in his opinion it served as a wake-up call. It told us we could be beaten even by a team we'd dominated. I think he's right. I know we took the entire postseason schedule very, very seriously. We had a lot to prove.

With that first game behind us, the coaches and most of the team were ready to keep on rolling. To win the national title, we had a series of tough games ahead of us, and no obstacle was going to stop us. We were finally going to learn if we were as good as our swagger, because in postseason you know everyone you face is going to be good. From that point on, every team we faced was a conference champion. Although our parade was going to be with a more elite group, we had intelligence, superior athletic ability, unity, determination, "the will to win," and a coach who was color-blind and wanted to win it all.

In some ways, Coach Haskins was in new territory. Coach Iba was quoted as saying, "I think Don [Haskins] thought we could beat Oklahoma City in the first game and we did. But when we were in Lubbock [for game two], we didn't know if we could get out of there, but I knew it."

All of our postseason games required that we travel some distance. More than one observer noted that El Paso wasn't close to anywhere. Lubbock was as near to home as we played. We'd played Texas Tech there before, and it was not a town friendly to us. Some 2,000 Texas Western fans made the trip, though, driving out in a long caravan of cars.

Fitzpatrick quotes Baudoin saying, "The tournament was actually a little easier for us because having to travel so much, we didn't have to practice as hard as we normally did. We were excited about possibly getting to see some other places. So we were kind of disappointed when we got sent to scenic Lubbock...." Lubbock was a tough place for black players to go. It was a pretty racist place then, and still is. But we knew we would be getting a chance to play some real good teams there. No more Eastern New Mexicos; finally we were going to play somebody who could challenge us."

WE HAD INTELLIGENCE, SUPERIOR ATHLETIC ABILITY, UNITY, DETERMINATION, "THE WILL TO WIN," AND A COACH WHO WAS COLOR-BLIND AND WANTED TO WIN IT ALL.

As I've noted, the Texas Western advantage as we advanced was that no one knew us. No one, including Kentucky, had bothered to scout us. Despite our remarkable season, no one took us seriously except the players and the city of El Paso. From my perspective, every team we were about to face was standing on the tracks while a train barreled down on them—and no one saw it coming.

We flew home for one day of practice then left for Lubbock, Texas, where we were to meet the University of Cincinnati, the Missouri Valley Conference champion, on Friday night. Cincinnati was a very good team, one of the most respected in the country. It was, I'm told, a great game to see and has been described as the most acrobatic of the NCAA Regionals. They were among the first of the major college programs to integrate, though its star was white, Don Rolfes.

Rolfes had originally played for Adolph Rupp at Kentucky, but he had married. Rupp apparently didn't approve of his players marrying. He wanted no distractions from basketball, so Rolfes had transferred to Cincinnati. Just before our game, he told a reporter that, "Playing against Kentucky for the national championship is something I have dreamed about."

To fulfill that dream, he had to get by us. That meant he was taking little old Texas Western for granted.

In the first five minutes of that game, something very unusual happened. Nevil Shed, normally a very quiet, soft-spoken, and controlled player, got into it with Rolfes under the basket. Rolfes had thrown an elbow into Shed that had really angered him. He responded by throwing a left hook at him, punching the guy in the nose, and was ejected from the game. I couldn't believe it.

Haskins was so angry that as soon as Shed got to the bench, he shouted, "You're through!" Then Coach Haskins chewed him out and told him to get off the floor. But when he tried to wait the game out in the locker room, the coach ordered him out of the building. Shed found a payphone and called home to tell his mother what happened, and she yelled at him worse than the coach had.

But it didn't do Rolfes any good.

Cincinnati tried to play man-to-man, and that was a big mistake. Though their center was a pretty good player, he simply wasn't effective against me. No one else was brave enough to try man-to-man against us the rest of play offs.

Still, we were behind the entire game, which drove our fans nuts. We finally pulled ahead with just two minutes left in the game, but at the final buzzer the game was tied.

We played that overtime tooth and nail. There was no room for error at this level. You couldn't turn the ball over, you couldn't make mistakes. It was a tough game. Willie Cager had missed a free throw with only seconds to go in the regular play and made up for it by scoring 6 of our 9 points in overtime.

I scored 29 points, because I was able to work against one guy all night who wasn't up to it. I also had eight rebounds. Rolfes only scored 10 points. The Texas Tech coach, Gene Gibson, watched the game. "I saw one smart guy from

Cincinnati," he told a reporter. "He was the one that saw Lattin coming and got the heck out of there."

Coach Haskins wrote later that we beat one great team, and he considered us lucky to have done it. I never considered us lucky. We were prepared, and we were the better team. He had done a great job getting us ready. If you depend on luck to win, you won't.

This was the game where I caught the eye of the national media for the first time. I had worked on my intimidation game all season, and Coach Haskins encouraged it in the whole team. Reporters wrote about us, and me in particular, as if we were urban street thugs, as likely to have a knife in our shorts as not. I was compared to heavyweight champion Sonny Liston as a scowling thug prone to violence. One wrote about my "treacherous strength and cold-blooded tactics," another described me as "a huge and awesome specimen." Inside I was just a young man, giving my absolute best to each performance, but if that's the way they saw me, so much the better. It made my job on the court that much easier.

When they called us a bunch of young men looking for a brawl, or bandits from the badlands, I took no offense. I knew they were referring to me.

Our final game, before we advanced to the Final Four, would be against the fourth-ranked team in the nation, Kansas. Fitzpatrick wrote that their coach, Ted Owens, lobbied the officials to crack down on us—that is, on me—saying to reporters, "We'll be all right, unless we get a loosely called game."

I don't know about that. What I know is what happened. The officials called 46 fouls, but it went against Kansas in the end. Flournoy fouled out on our team, but Walt Wesley, Jo Jo White, and Ron Franz all did on the Kansas team.

Kansas had won the Big Eight, and going in we knew they had to be taken seriously. They were also big guys and very hard to defend. It was the teams with big players that had given us the most trouble all year. Their center, Walt Wesley, was just barely under seven feet tall and was huge. He looked down on me like I was a little boy, like he was thinking there was no way I was going to give him any trouble. He was very strong and I had to work on him the entire game. I could tell they worked out with weights. It really showed.

If I've given the impression I was the only intimidator on the team, consider this: In that game, Flournoy blocked Walt Wesley, the Kansas All-American, when he attempted to dunk. As they dropped to the court, Flournoy smirked and called Wesley a "sissy."

In addition to being big and strong, they were a well-balanced team with a great bench, but they'd not played against a team like us all year. They had fewer opportunities to take good shots than they were used to, and I'm sure they found it frustrating. When they would get a shot off, they weren't likely to get a rebound. Given the way we played, it just wasn't in the cards.

But this was a hard-fought game between two teams of nearly equal talent and commitment. I've always believed that we were the better team, because we had more desire to win. The first half the game was tied ten times, and the lead changed hands four times. Our biggest lead was five points, theirs was four. Flournoy tipped two balls in a row into the basket at the end of the first half to give us the halftime lead, 38-35.

In the second half, Kansas switched to a stall in an attempt to offset our quickness. Slowing the game down was, for them, a critical error. Bobby Joe and Orsten started stealing the ball and shooting layups. We were leading by 5 points with just over a minute to go when I went up and dunked the ball. That should have been the end of the game.

To keep from taking a potentially injury-causing fall, I hung longer on the rim than the referees liked; the points were disallowed, and I was called for a technical. Whoever blew the whistle didn't see the player standing just below me. But working as I did up against the rim, dunking balls with force, was very new to basketball, and the referees were generally uncomfortable with the rules about what was and was not allowed.

Then White stole a ball and, with a penalty, scored three points, tying the game with half a minute to go. Bobby Joe got in the last shot, but it missed, forcing us into a second overtime in as many games.

The first overtime period was all defense, with each of us only scoring two points apiece. I pulled down every rebound at both ends of the court. Kansas had a shot at winning, but what followed was another moment of controversy. White made a 25-foot shot in the final seconds.

I didn't know what was taking place on the sidelines. I just saw the shot drop through and screamed at Bobby Joe, "Judge! I don't believe it! You let the guy shoot that? You didn't smack him in the head?"

"Chill, Judge," Bobby Joe said, knowing the shot was no good.

Kansas thought they had won, but Bobby Joe was all over White; the only way he could get clear to attempt the shot was to step back out of bounds. It didn't count. The referee immediately went down to one knee and pointed to the spot where White's foot was out of bounds. On a tape of the game, you could clearly see it.

"It was," as Worsley wisely told a reporter later, "the most important moment in Texas Western's history, right there."

The call took the steam out of Kansas. For a moment they thought that they had won, then they had to reconcile to a second tie. That's a real mood swing for any young team to make. They just weren't ready for us when the game resumed. In the second overtime, we got the lead and put them in a position of having to come back. At the end they needed three and could only make two with their final attempts.

We won, 81-80. Bobby Joe scored 22 points to my 15 with 17 rebounds. Nevil, coming into the game from the bench, still scored 12 and stopped Wesley, limiting him to 24 points though he shot thirty-five times to do it. White had 19 points.

> THEY WERE GOOD TEAMS, GREAT EVEN, BUT WE WERE GREATER STILL.

As we walked off the court, I could hear Kansas players saying, "We had them! We had them! We should have won that game!" I had heard the same talk from the Cincinnati players after that game. Sure, both games were close, but we would have beaten them in any rematch. They were good teams, great even, but we were greater still. Against them, we always played well enough to win. Maybe we were too confident, even cocky. Coach Haskins certainly thought so. I just knew that this was our fourth overtime game that season, the first to go double overtime, and we won all four.

Coach Haskins was understandably upset, saying we tried to give the game away, though he acknowledged that we looked good doing it. But he didn't yell at us for the game being so close. Sometimes, after a close game like that, he would start to yell, but a friend would remind him we had won. Frankly, this wasn't the first time we'd won so close a game. I know it drove him nuts when we'd play like that. As for us, we'd never doubted for a second that we were going to win that game.

Bobby Joe polled 79 points out of a possible 80 to make the first team all-tournament. I got 76 votes, and also had the honor of being on the first team. The most points scored by a player in the tournament was 47. I scored 44 and was a close second. My individual score of 29 in one game was the best in the tournament. I also came in second with 25 rebounds. In head-to-head competition, I out-rebounded the winner 17 to 15, by two rebounds. Bobby Joe was selected Most Valuable Player. What was most important is we had the win.

Kansas was a very fine team, and some have said it was the best team we played all year. They were awfully good, better against us than either Utah or Kentucky proved to be. But they were a bit slow, and had they gone on to face Kentucky, I'm not so certain they would have won. Kentucky's style of play would probably have been more effective against them than it turned out to be against us.

We felt, and I believe Coach Haskins and Coach Iba felt, the worst was behind us. Our first opponent in the Final Four was Utah, and their star center had just broken his leg. The national press gave neither Utah nor Texas Western any respect, figuring the national title was going to be decided with the preliminary game between Duke and Kentucky.

We agreed, at least partially. We didn't think Utah was going to be a problem for us. And from what little we knew of Duke and Kentucky, they were small teams. The ones that had given us a real problem all year had been those with big players who played a physical game. So as we advanced to the Final Four, we were very, very confident.

We weren't alone. Teams we had beaten knew how good we were, and so did their coaches. Kansas coach Ted Owens said, "We felt the best teams in the country had played that night. We didn't feel Kentucky had enough size."

So with that win, we advanced to the Final Four. Duke and Kentucky both had segregated teams, though I didn't know that at the time.

CHAPTER 10

MUSHROOM EFFECT

Kentucky was playing for a commemorative wristwatch and the right to say they were national champions. We were out to prove that it didn't matter what color a person's skin was.

TEXAS WESTERN'S HARRY FLOURNOY

FRANKLY, I DIDN'T PAY much attention to Kentucky during that season, and I don't recall that I'd ever heard of Adolph Rupp until then. As we entered the top ten in the national rankings, and as, one by one, the other undefeated teams took a loss, we rose in the ratings. It was about then we started following Kentucky, especially when we were the only two remaining teams without a loss.

Basketball, as I understand it, is like a religion in Kentucky. I'm told that if you aren't a college basketball fan when you move there, you will soon become one.

If there was a high priest of basketball in Kentucky, it was Adolph Rupp. The season of 1965-66 was towards the end of his career. He was sixty-four years old, and there was talk that his best days were behind him. His team had a miserable season the previous year, and he was highly motivated to put together a great team from what was a very talented but undersized squad. I'm sure he always wanted to win the title—every coach and player does at the start of the season—but he also wanted to silence his critics.

He did a good job, as their record shows. The team could pass, shoot, play defense, and even rebound despite their size. They depended on the fast break, which in turn relied on defensive rebounding, and they were deadly from outside, though I've always been partial to the saying about "living and dying" with outside jump shots. Nothing beats a good inside game, and no move silences an opponent like an aggressive dunk. The Kentucky Wildcats were highly disciplined and played unselfishly, similar to us.

My matchup was to be against Thad Jaracz. He was six feet, five inches tall, shorter than I was, and 230 pounds, about my weight. Rupp would have preferred another center, but he just didn't have one; he worked Jaracz hard to mold him into the player he needed.

Though Kentucky was an all-white team, some of the schools they played were integrating. That season, of the twenty-seven regular games they played, they faced no more than twelve black players. Great black players came out of Kentucky, some even played for Kentucky schools, but they made winners out of other colleges.

Kentucky fans are rabid, I'm told, and every home game was a sellout. I can only imagine the excitement as the team remained undefeated against tough opponents. I had a great taste of the same thing in El Paso, though our fans weren't used to it like theirs were. They easily won their first game that season, 83-55, against Hardin-Simmons of Texas. But the words of their coach were prophetic, in my opinion. He said of

Kentucky, "That's a good little team, [but] when it runs into a big boy, it's going to have trouble." Words to live by, especially when you're the big boy.

Rupp's Runts always looked to run. Given their size, what choice did they have? Larry Conley is quoted by Fitzpatrick saying, "If we had to go to a half-court game, we knew we would be in a lot of trouble because teams were bigger than us and we couldn't pound it inside. We had to get shots from the outside or get it off the break. So as soon as we got the ball it looked like an all-out blitz, five guys running to the other end. But we almost always got it into the hands of the right people."

Kentucky beat Virginia and Illinois early on with Jaracz scoring 54 points. During the early part of the season, they were scarcely challenged, winning their first six games by an average of 23 points. Fitzpatrick quotes Tommy Kron saying, "We started out winning games so easily. We were whipping people down big-time. We'd take a 15 point lead and extend it to 30. It seemed we got stronger as the games wore on and part of that was our new conditioning program, the weights and especially the running."

By their eleventh game, Kentucky was already ranked number one. They had their only scare the last game of the regular season, this against Georgia, who took them into double overtime before finally losing. Tommy Kron said, "It was about then that we started to say to each other, 'Hey, we're really playing well together.' Every one of us was on a roll. All five of us knew who was going to take the shot if all of us were open—Louie [Dampier] or Pat [Riley]. Everybody knew that when the ball went up certain people would go get it. Everybody knew that when there was a tough guy to guard, he was mine.... Everybody knew if we were running a play, I would start it so that Louie could end up on the shooting end of it. Before long we were 10-0 and it had a sort of mushroom effect."

For all their size problems, they still out-rebounded opponents, only losing in the stats five times that regular season. No wonder their fast break worked, since it feeds off the rebound.

Like us, Rupp preferred that his Wildcats play man-to-man defense, but unlike us, he had a zone he regularly employed when the man-to-man wasn't working. It was an unusual 1-3-1 zone trap. He picked it because few teams ran across it, and it could be confusing until you figured it out. It had the capacity to disrupt the flow of a game, and if you're having trouble, that's exactly what you want to do. It allegedly forced bad passes, and you couldn't effectively drive to the basket against it. Kentucky used it sparingly, because the reality was that once a team showed it a few times, most teams could tear it apart pretty fast. Still, they employed it effectively that year, most notably against Texas Tech, who had big players giving them trouble. They came from behind using the 1-3-1 zone defense.

After twenty-three undefeated games, Kentucky had taken the Southeast Conference title. The same day we took our only defeat of the year against Seattle, the Wildcats faced Tennessee for their second-to-last regular season game. Tennessee was their arch rival, and they had beaten them badly at home the previous week, 78-64, just as we had beaten Seattle earlier. They lost the second game, 69-62, and sent us onto the court to face Seattle overconfident, but coming away from the game with a wake-up call. Kentucky went on to stomp Tulane in their last game of the regular season, scoring 103 points.

Kentucky advanced to the Mideast Regional to be played that year in Iowa City. Their first game was against Dayton, and they had a rough first half. The Dayton center was just under seven feet tall, and his size gave the Wildcats considerable

PREPARATION MAKES ALL THE DIFFERENCE IN THE WORLD.

trouble, but they turned the game around with their patented 1-3-1 zone defense. Though the center ended up with 36 points, the rest of the team didn't fare so well, and Kentucky won 86-79. Dampier scored 34 points while Riley had 29.

Life can be unfair, and the same is so in basketball. Players can end up playing an entire season with a nagging injury that reduces their effectiveness. A key player can break a bone and not be available, just when you need him the most. A team can catch a cold. To win it all you need talent, skill, and a bit of luck. The reality is that everyone in collegiate basketball, and every team, over the course of a season, faces about the same level of adversity. It can skew one way or another, but we all have to deal with issues that affect play. Preparation makes all the difference in the world.

Fitzpatrick, and others, have written about a cold some of the Kentucky players caught about that time. The story goes they next played Michigan with two players, Conley and Jaracz, feeling under the weather. It was another tough game, won 84-77, apparently by Dampier and Riley's key outside shooting down the stretch. But afterwards, as the team arrived in Lexington, players had scratchy throats, the chills, and sniffles.

Still, the team was elated to be in the Final Four. They had won twenty-six out of twenty-seven games. "Nobody could have foreseen this," Rupp said. "You could only dream about it. [It] is a simply unbelievable record when you stop and think about it."

The Kentucky Wildcats flew to Baltimore on Thursday, then took the bus to the Sheraton Motor Inn in Silver Spring, Maryland, where they and a large contingent of their boosters were staying. They were scheduled to play number two Duke on Friday night, just after our game against Utah.

Our final defeat in Seattle had worked a miracle in the ratings. We had been number two, but in our loss slipped to third place. Duke leapfrogged over us and guess what?— Kentucky, with a loss, got to stay number one. Imagine that.

The Final Four games were scheduled at College Park, and pretty much everyone figured Kentucky and Duke were playing for the title. Whichever team the winner faced Saturday night would be a walkover. The writer for the nearby *Washington Post* wrote that this was the "game the nation has been squirming for," as if we and Utah weren't to be considered. A major college coach was quoted voicing the sentiments of the national media, saying, "I think the finals are going to be played Friday night."

The two teams played a great game. I watched it. Fitzpatrick writes that the game was tied six times between scores 61-61 and 71-71. That sounds about right. With a score of 83-79, Kentucky won it. One observer, according to Fitzpatrick, commented that the game between two all-white teams had likely marked a bit of history as it would probably be the last significant NCAA game with two white teams, to which I said, "Amen."

CHAPTER 11

CHANGING EVERYTHING

The running, gunning Texas quintet

can do more things with a basketball

than a monkey on a 50-foot wire.

JAMES H. JACKSON,
Baltimore Sun

WE WERE CALLED LUCKY to have come this far. I've often wondered that if Cincinnati had won that overtime period against us and ended up in the Final Four, would any sportswriter have called them lucky? How about Kansas? What if White hadn't stepped out of bounds and they had won that game in the first overtime period? Would anyone have called them lucky?

You make your luck in situations like that. We had beaten really good teams all season and since the NCAA play offs began, not because we were lucky but because we were better. Yet no one outside of El Paso seemed willing to admit it.

Fitzpatrick quotes Louis Baudoin saying, "The mood on the club going into the tournament was anger." When I say we advanced to the championship series with something to prove, you can believe it.

We spent an exciting week in El Paso, practicing as we always did, before traveling to College Park, Maryland, for the Final Four play. It wasn't just the student body, boosters, or local fans who were excited; we were going to be on national television for the first time and be exposed to the world. We were all excited at the prospect. For a lot of us, this would be the first time our family and friends had a chance to see us play at this level, and they were going to see us on a very big stage. We'd been trying to prove something all year and really hadn't been able to. Now we had our chance. All we had to do was keep winning.

That week, *Sports Illustrated* published an article about the upcoming championship series. Speaking of Utah initially, the article said, "...They must face Western's David Lattin, who is six foot seven and the best unknown ballplayer in the country. Lattin anchors a team that is the nation's roughest.... And the mere presence of Lattin would be enough to intimidate most teams. He has the stark, forbidding scowl of the vintage Liston, plus smooth, agile movements that belie his size. 'He is the only man,' Haskins says plainly enough, 'who ever made Jim Barnes cower...yes, cower.'"

We knew we would be playing Utah first and that they had knocked off the New Mexico Lobos who'd given us so much trouble. But the Utah center had broken his leg and wouldn't be playing in the game. Frankly, I've always been disappointed about that. I heard he was very good and would really have liked to have played against him.

As it was, Utah was not expected to put up much of a fight. Not that it mattered. Everyone acted as if the "real" game was to be played Friday night between Kentucky and Duke. Whichever team won between Utah and Texas Western would be murdered in the final game. They had no absolutely no chance.

Coach Iba had long since run out of scouting money. I think he had something like $5,000 a season to spend. I doubt he or Coach Haskins ever expected us to go this far, so if other arrangements could have been made, they weren't. It happened that Coach Haskins had seen Utah in practice during the preseason and knew their coach, Jack Gardner, very well. He knew that Utah was a fast-break team, that they worked hard at it in their drills, not necessarily to score off the fast break initially but rather to set the pace of the game, to get the opposing team into that rhythm. If such a team can do that, they are very close to winning the game.

That week, our coaches talked to us about Utah and how we should prepare. Our drills were structured around making certain at least two players got back on defense under our basket so Utah would not be unchallenged on the break, but by this point in the season there really wasn't all that much a coach could do for his team. He had either prepared us, or he hadn't. We were cautioned about Utah's great star, Jerry Chambers, and knew we had to contain him to win. He scored 73 points in the two games before that Friday night.

The lead-up to the NCAA finals took place in the days before ESPN, cable television, recruiting bureaus, or widespread summer camps, so it was not unexpected that we arrived in Maryland as a virtual unknown, one reporter calling us "an intriguing rumor." Our great advantage all season had been that no one knew us, and it remained our advantage for those final two games.

We'd played our share of weak teams and had beaten some really fine opponents like Iowa and Kansas, teams known to the sportswriters. Still, no national reporter expected us to finish any better than as a so-so-run, either Friday night against Utah or Saturday against whichever team we faced. It was the consensus that the championship game was to be played that Friday night between all-white Duke and all-white Kentucky.

Texas Western was allotted just 250 tickets, and they all sold out. Since so few could attend in person, a local television station in El Paso arranged to broadcast the game live and in color. Our 250 fans from El Paso were swallowed up in the enormous Cole Field House, with a seating capacity of 14,000, located on the campus of the University of Maryland. I wasn't bothered by this, since I knew we required no fans to win. We had the band and our cheerleading squad, and Bobby Joe's family and friends came down from New York City to watch us play. That was our cheering section. Bobby Joe was really excited about having his folks there, about them having the chance to see him play in such a great event. His entourage included many friends and his older brother, whom he'd always looked up to.

> I DON'T BELIEVE ONE OF US WAS INTIMIDATED BY THE EVENT OR THE CROWD.

I don't believe one of us was intimidated by the event or the crowd. Willie Worsley told Fitzpatrick, "There really wasn't a lot of hype among our guys. Maybe we were just old for our age because of our life experiences. And remember in my high school career, I had played before 18,000 people in Madison Square Garden. Being from New York City, and being MVP in the city championship game, playing in the Garden was my greatest thrill. After that, everything was anticlimactic."

We arrived at College Park on St. Patrick's Day, three days before the championship game. On the flight, we had all been given green string ties to wear. Commenting that his name wasn't "Mick," Nevil Shed said he would wear one anyway. We stayed at the same hotel as Duke and felt like interlopers in the midst of a sea of fans. They were everywhere, just as excited as people can get. Stretched across the front windows of the hotel was an enormous banner, LET'S GO DUKE. The excitement at the prospect of another national championship was written on every face.

I watched it with a certain measure of bemusement. We hadn't come this far to not win it all. That was something these fans were about to discover.

A record number of sportswriters, 150, had requested credentials to cover the tournament. The first fifteen minutes of our practice the day we arrived were open to the media, and for nearly all of them, that was the first time they realized the Miners had so many black players. More than one looked to see where we were from, and Fitzpatrick reports there was already talk that the team had been recruited by cheating.

I guess it wasn't one of our better practices—that's what Coach Haskins says about it—but then he always thought we were lazy in practice. He yanked Bobby Joe off the court and sent him to the showers. At one point he shouted towards the reporters, "Isn't this the laziest bunch you've ever seen?"

Once in Maryland, we were largely in a bubble, but we still began to hear things about ourselves from the national sportswriters there, that we "were a bunch of angry young men looking for a brawl."

Willie Worsley said, "We were number three and we ought to have gotten our just dues. The papers were filled with stuff about Duke and Kentucky and their All-Americans. We didn't have any All-Americans. We felt a little left out. Pat Riley was from the East and so were some of us, but guess who got all the ink?" Worsley was off the mark about the team's All-Americans—Bobby Joe and I were both All-American that year—but he was right about us being ignored.

For all the final game had come to mean, there was no sense entering the finals thinking that this was going to be a racial matchup. Willie Worsley felt the same as I believe we all did. He told Fitzpatrick, "There's no way we went into that game thinking this would be great for blacks. Why should we? Who knows when they're going to make history? At that time, we didn't know it. We all had our own little set of priorities. Me personally, I knew nothing about Rupp. I didn't know who was coaching for Kentucky. And you can ask me now and I still can't tell you who coached Duke. We knew they were segregated. We were a very clever and intelligent team as Coach Haskins often said. But Rupp didn't wear a uniform. He wasn't the one who was going to run by me."

But race was a part of it at some level, no matter how some wanted to make light of it later. The black players on my team stuck out in a hotel otherwise filled to overflowing with whites. Our coaches knew race was a factor. Not long before that final game, I read that Coach Haskins and Moe Iba went out to eat. As they were walking to the hotel, Coach Haskins asked Iba, "You think they'll let us win it?" Now maybe he was concerned because we were new to this level of competition, or maybe it was because his starters were African-American.

Later Coach Haskins said, "I knew who we were. I knew who Kentucky was and what it represented." Kentucky had paid their dues. They were respected. They were expected to win, while Texas Western came from obscurity and could just as easily fade back into it, with a little help if necessary.

For some months we had been called the Miracle Miners. The name was part tribute to our phenomenal season and reaching the Final Four, part statement it would take a miracle for us to win it all.

The Utah game demonstrated to me just how precarious any eventual championship could be. I personally had absolutely no doubt we could beat the slower Utah team, especially without their starting center. The Utah coach made the usual plea coaches who feared me did. He said, "They're like a pro team around the boards. They throw their weight around and they're all leapers. All we have is a bunch of skinny little kids." To another reporter he said, "They play like a professional team. Their board play is their strongest asset. They take you in deep and stack their offense under the basket. They've got the personnel to get the job done." I elected to stay out of the way of players who drove for or reached the board.

My precautions and careful play didn't work. The referees called twenty-seven fouls on us, and early in the second half, I drew my fourth and had to sit down. I told a reporter later that they were calling it like a "girl's game." I still think they were. Nevil agreed. "They called baby fouls."

We led by three at the half when I was in the game. The one player giving us fits was Jerry Chambers. Now follow this next part: You remember that great bench we had? How they made us work hard in practice? How little drop-off in skill took place when they came in? With me down, Coach Haskins sent in six feet, four inch, and white, Jerry Armstrong. What Jerry did was work at keeping the ball out of Chambers' hands. He deflected passes, got his hand at them even when he didn't touch them. And if Chambers didn't have the ball, he couldn't score. Chambers had a great night regardless, scoring 38 points, the most of any by a single player against a Miner team since Coach Haskins had arrived. But Jerry slowed the guy way down in the second half. Once Jerry was in, Utah never challenged us for the lead, and we won 85-78.

Jerry Armstrong said afterwards that sitting on the bench for the first half had been a big advantage for him. He had studied Chambers carefully. "So when I came in I had a good idea of where Chambers was going to move and what he would try to do." And, of course, he had the talent to do what he needed to do.

The matchup was crucial, and more than one player on our team gave Jerry his well-deserved credit. It's been written that without him we would have never played Kentucky the next night. Maybe. But if the referees hadn't put me on the bench with a bunch of terrible calls who's to say how it would have shaken down. The point is that the quality of that team was such that we had him when we needed him. Still, it was a sobering experience and a reminder that being the better team didn't necessarily mean we were going to win.

After the game, I was in no mood to celebrate. I quickly showered, then hurried out to watch the Duke-Kentucky game. I had never seen either of them play before, and this was my only opportunity to conduct my own scouting. Throughout the season, I had felt that the job of winning rested on my shoulders alone. It was likely that Bobby Joe felt the same way.

As I stood to the side and watched the teams during warm-up, I was struck with the sight and stood for a moment in wonder. Every player was white! Until then I'd had no idea the teams were not integrated, or if I had, the realization hadn't sunk in. There was a stirring inside me that I couldn't quite pin down.

At that moment, as I prepared for the game, I knew something profound was about to take place. Here we were, the Texas Western Miners, and here they were, whichever team won this game, an all-white team who would play us. Some part of me understood, or sensed, that we were on a collision course.

The second thing I noticed was that both Duke and Kentucky were the same size as the Miners. Neither of them had a big center, neither had two or three big guys to crowd up the center and get in my way. All season, the teams that had given us the most trouble had been the ones with big players. It was then I knew with absolute certainty that we could beat either team.

Next I watched the centers they *had*, the players I would be on. Was the center a rebounder, a shot blocker? What I saw was that both teams were jump shooters and weren't really trying to go inside. This was a revelation. What it meant was that I didn't have to worry about guarding my man that closely. This would allow me to roam and help my teammates in ways that had been limited all season.

As I stood there unobserved on the sidelines, I planned for the strategic and tactical side of the next night's game, how I would play, block shots, rebound, and score points to help my team win.

As I watched, I realized I didn't see a single dunk by any player. It wasn't the style of play for either of them, assuming anyone on either team could do it. Well, whichever team we faced was about to have a learning session. As I left the floor, I had only one chilling concern: Would the white referees let us win?

I joined Bobby Joe and went with him and his family to dinner. As we chatted away, I sat there calm and confident. Whichever team we faced the next night, we owned, God willing.

I read later that the Duke-Kentucky game was great. At one point, the game was tied six times. Kentucky won, 83-79. The *Washington Post* rather prematurely referred to the victory as "the perfect end of the long season" for Kentucky.

Adolf Rupp spent the day before the final game in Washington D.C., accepting various Coach of the Year awards from a gathering of basketball sportswriters. Rupp had been voted Coach of Year by UPI with a record 163 votes, while Coach Haskins had received just 12 votes. After the function, Coach Haskins commented that he didn't think Rupp even knew who he was. The talk in the various hospitality rooms was that we didn't have a chance.

That week and at the tournament, Coach Haskins seemed pretty normal to me, though others have written about how nervous he was. He understood, I know, that he might never get into the championship game again in his career. Most college coaches never play for it all; now here he was, preparing to go against a basketball legend, Adolph Rupp, and a great team. "Mr. Rupp is 64," he told a reporter, "and he's made it lots of times. It's probably going to be just once in a lifetime for me."

He was right. He got there just that one time, but no one can say he didn't make his mark. I'll take Coach Haskins' single win to Adolph Rupp's four anytime.

The El Paso sportswriters were already calling the Utah victory enough, as if they expected our defeat that night.

The Associated Press had written, "Texas Western is even bigger and rougher than Duke [who gave Kentucky so much trouble], but that may be the downfall of the Miners against a team with the finesse and discipline of Kentucky."

Let's get this right: Duke nearly beat Kentucky, and Texas Western was "bigger and rougher," but we were going to lose because Kentucky had more finesse (compared to our lack of it) and discipline (compared to our undisciplined play). I doubt that reporter had ever seen us play.

If the national sportswriters, even our own sportswriters, saw Kentucky as preordained, there were dissenters, and not just in our locker room. Coaches whose teams had played us or knew our program didn't give Kentucky much of a chance. Jimmy Viramontes of West Texas State told a Texas reporter, "Kentucky can't play Texas Western man-to-man. They have no one who can stay with Bobby Joe Hill and David Lattin." The SMU coach Doc Hayes said, "I said from the first I thought Texas Western would win. It has the strongest defense, a great driver and ball handler [Hill], a good outside shooter [Artis], a tough rebounder [Lattin], and is tremendously well disciplined as a team." Either the Associated Press writer didn't hear this or didn't believe it.

It's been written that with his victory over Duke, Adolph Rupp thought the worst was behind him. With their win, it was generally believed that Kentucky had sewn up the national championship. All that remained was a walkover of the upstarts from El Paso. At a gathering, and reflecting what I think was a commonly held belief by many Americans at the time, Rupp told reporters that no five Negro players could beat his five white players. It was impossible. Maybe he didn't use the word "Negro." I'm not sure. Then he guaranteed that Kentucky would beat Texas Western that night. It's also been written that he didn't say it at the tournament, but on the radio in Kentucky the previous week. How he knew that he would be playing us then is beyond me, but what is agreed is that he said it.

There is another aspect to this game that was surely on Adolph Rupp's mind, at least that's what I've read. John Wooden at UCLA had won the national title the previous two years. Lew Alcindor, later to become Kareem Abdul-Jabbar, had just finished his freshman year at UCLA and would play on the varsity squad the next year. It was generally held that UCLA was the favorite to sweep three titles in a row. They did, plus four more. It is said that Adolph Rupp knew this would be his last real shot at title number five. Going into his game against us, Adolph Rupp had won 749 games in his storied career. We were to have been number seven hundred and fifty.

Earlier that day in the hotel room, Bobby Joe and I talked about the coming game, discussing its significance now that we realized we were about to play an all-white team. "We're not losing. Absolutely, positively not," I said, echoing Bobby Joe.

The team met in the hotel restaurant for our traditional pre-game meal at about three that Saturday afternoon. In those days it was steak and potatoes, with the emphasis on steak. We ate this early so no one would cramp up during the game. I think most teams did it that way.

WE ALWAYS FORCED THE OTHER TEAMS TO PLAY *OUR* GAME. THIS WAS GOING TO BE NO DIFFERENT.

At some point, I mentioned to Coach Haskins that I had watched some of the game the night before. He expressed surprised to see that I had taken the time and effort to do it. He and Coach Iba had watched the entire game.

Not much later, Coach Haskins met with the African American players alone, for the usual pre-game chalk talk. We gathered in my room, which I was sharing with Bobby Joe. Fitzpatrick had written that Coach Haskins found us "typically unconcerned." He was expecting us to be as on edge as I guess he was. We had driven the poor man nuts all season with our cocky attitudes. I guess this really got to him.

There we were, lounging about, hands in back of our heads, Bobby Joe twirling a toothpick in his mouth. The coach tried telling us how good Kentucky was, that we shouldn't take them for granted, that this one game was for it all, but he didn't get any reaction out of us. He didn't have much to say about how Kentucky played, because he hadn't scouted them until the night before. We were veteran players by this point and used to winning. No changes were needed. We played every game the same way nearly all season; the system was working. We always forced the other teams to play *our* game. This was going to be no different.

About our attitude, Willie Worsley might have said it best: "Sure, we might have been cocky, but we were all from places— New York, Detroit, Indiana, Chicago—where you had to be cocky [carry a certain confidence] to survive." He might have mentioned Houston, too. "We knew Kentucky was a good team, we weren't going to overlook them. But we felt we could beat them. If you would have seen us that afternoon, you'd have thought we just had a pickup game that night. You would have thought that we thought we could walk on water."

Many years later, Coach Haskins seemed to understand us a bit better. He wrote that when you play for Kentucky you are expected to win, and win the national championship. That's where the pressure is. When you play for Texas Western, you have nothing to lose. I was firmly of the opinion we were going to win this game, and I wasn't alone. But he had it right. We were already a huge success. Just getting into this final game by itself would have been seen as more than enough. But we had no intention of just showing up.

Coach Haskins has also written that he was hearing this story about Adolph Rupp telling a joke that day that went this way: "What does TWC stand for? Two white coaches." He didn't tell us that one, but it was then Coach Haskins told us what Adolph Rupp had said, that there was no way black players could beat his white team. He had to know it would affect us; that's why he said it. He then paused to let it sink in. "It's up to you," he said, then left.

I looked at Bobby Joe and said, "He couldn't really have said that, could he?" Our eyes all met, and then the others filed out of the room. We knew what we had to do. We weren't going to lose. How could I go back to Houston and play ball if I let them beat us?

Fitzpatrick wrote in his first book that as we all rode over to the arena to get ready for the game, someone sat down next to the Texas Western president, Joe Ray, who'd brought Coach Haskins on board. This unnamed man is reported to have said, "Don't worry, Dr. Ray. We're going to win." Ray asked how he knew. "Cause those [black guys] there won't let those white boys beat 'em."

There was a great deal those sportswriters and others were ignoring, because the impending game was played in the very eye of the American Civil Rights Movement and the violence that went with it. Three years before our game that night, James Meredith had enrolled at Mississippi—with the help and protection of the National Guard. Malcolm X had been assassinated just the previous year. The marches in Selma, Alabama, were underway, with arrests of black leaders including Dr. Martin Luther King Jr.. Fire hoses were routinely turned on nonviolent black marchers, dogs were released on terrified protestors, shots fired in ambush.

The previous August, Congress had passed the Voting Rights Act, which had been followed by riots in Watts in Los Angeles. Twenty thousand National Guardsmen were turned out, 34 people were killed, 2,200 arrested and $200 million worth of property was destroyed. The Presidential order establishing Affirmative Action was issued in September. The Black Panthers were founded that fall, and in April, 1966, just a few weeks after the tournament, Stokely Carmichael coined the phrase "black power." The war in Vietnam was escalating, while overhead the Gemini astronauts were performing the first space walks. Just weeks before the game, Dr. King launched a civil rights campaign in Chicago. Mention of race in such a situation was considered tantamount to yelling fire in the crowded theater of America's cities, so the news articles before the game pretended the issue didn't exist.

When the bus stopped at the arena, we got out and gathered to collect our things. The white driver got out to hand everybody their bags. As he handed me mine, he looked at me and said, "Why are you guys even playing this game? You don't actually think you can beat Kentucky and Adolf Rupp? Why waste your time even going into the arena?"

I didn't answer the man. I just took my bag and walked away.

I've always thought that Bobby Joe said it best about that game. Here's his wisdom: "Everyone got it wrong.... It was Kentucky that was different, not us, not Texas Western." The fact was that most colleges were integrated and that the nation as a whole was ending segregation. All-white teams like Kentucky were dinosaurs.

We entered the arena at about eight o'clock, just as Duke and Utah were tipping off the consolation game. To appreciate the scene, consider for a moment an alternative reality. Imagine an all-black crowd, with all-black sportswriters, and black referees along with the Texas Western team. Now think about that all-white team entering and playing in such an environment. How would they have felt? How would they have performed?

I mention this because that's what it was like for us. My thoughts from the night before came back to me. *Were they, the white referees, going to let us win?* I had to stay in this game for us to have a shot at it, but I knew my ability to stay in the game was frankly out of my hands. It rested in the hearts and with the good will of those two referees, Steve Honzo and Thornton Jenkins.

The precedent-setting aspect of what was to come was not about Texas Western having black players. It was not unheard of for integrated teams to appear in the NCAA championship game. Cincinnati had won playing some blacks in 1961 and 1962, as did Loyola in 1963. They had started two, three, even four black players, but not five.

As we dressed, Coach Haskins stood outside in the hallway and was approached by reporters. I guess they wanted to know why he wasn't with his team. Always frank, he said, "I'm tired of looking at the players and they're tired of looking at me." Like I've said, we drove that poor man crazy that season.

It's been written, and hinted at a lot, that Adolph Rupp didn't take us seriously because Coach Haskins started five black players and played a largely black team. I don't know about that, but I'm willing to say this; I don't think he took us seriously because we were from lowly Texas Western, in the sagebrush part of Texas, a state not known for great college basketball. He was the Baron of the Bluegrass, the creator of the greatest college basketball program in history to that point. We were nobodies, we didn't count. And I say all that as a proud Texan.

Coach Haskins had this game scoped out very differently from the national sportswriters, according to Fitzpatrick. Texas Western's secret weapon was me. "David didn't score a lot of points, but the one thing he did was he could be very intimidating inside. He was like 6-6, 240, and a great jumper. And I don't think Kentucky had ever played against anyone like him, someone who could dominate them." He and I were on the same page because I *knew* those boys had never faced anyone like me before.

Coach Haskins understood that Rupp liked for his teams to run and gun. He had seen some of that the night before. He also knew that Kentucky had an excellent offense and was used to scoring a lot of points to win its games. He discussed his thoughts with Coach Iba and said we needed to pick up the ball when Kentucky tried to break. The strategy was the same as it had been for us all season, that is, get the opposing team out of their game plan.

Once we were dressed, Coach Haskins entered the dressing room. Four who usually started got the nod to start that night; these were Bobby Joe, Orsten, Flournoy, and me. No surprise. Then he said that "Willie" would be the fifth player. Hearing this, Willie Worsley patted Willie Cager on the back. "No, little man," Coach Haskins said, "I mean you." Kentucky was small and quick, so Coach Haskins had decided to go with three guards who would all drop back to protect the basket against the fast break. That left just two of us to rebound. Otherwise that meant that Willie was going to guard six feet, three inch Larry Conley.

Another advantage of three guards was that we could take our time bringing the ball up the court. This would keep Kentucky from setting the tempo of the game, something very important for the run-and-gun style they played. All three of these guards were excellent ball handlers. Kentucky gained nothing by trying to focus on Bobby Joe, for example. He would just pass the ball to Willie or to Orsten; all three guards played the entire game.

The crowd of 14,000 that Saturday night was almost entirely composed of Kentucky fans. After I was dressed, and as I stood waiting to go on the court for warm-up, I tried to take it all in. I had never seen so many people in a place before, and everyone was white: the fans, the referees, the reporters. Even the bus drivers were white, and the guy who sold hotdogs. White, white, white.

I stood there watching the pre-game festivities and immediately spotted Confederate battle flags dotting the all-white crowd. Then the Kentucky band struck up Dixie, and a cheerleader ran around the arena brandishing an enormous Confederate flag to the rousing cheers of the crowd.

This wasn't the first all-white team I had ever played, not even the first I'd played against that year. But those games had always been athletic struggles with no time to consider the color of someone's skin or even if it was relevant.

But something about this was different. That was what I had been sensing the previous night. There was a culture on display here. These fans reveled in it unquestioningly. As I stood there, watching the frenzied crowd, I suddenly understood that in their view this was to be a racist contest. In their minds there was absolutely no doubt which was the better race, no doubt at all as to who would win. Something deep within my soul stirred, such as I had never experienced before, nor have experienced since.

Listening to Dixie, watching that enormous Confederate battle flag, I understood what this display of raw racism was meant to be. Kentucky was figuratively, and literally, carrying the banner for the white racists of America.

I watched the Kentucky crowd getting whipped up, jumping up and down in their seats, all but unable to contain their excitement.

In those defining moments, I fully understood what was at stake, and I instinctively grasped what a defeat would mean. We could not afford to lose. Black Americans could not stand the setback of a defeat. I could not go home if we lost this game. I could not go there ever again and hold my head up. My teammates and I had a part to play in the epic struggle on the streets that until this night had seemed so distant. Our part for the Cause was here, this night, amidst this ocean of white racism. We couldn't lose.

During warm-up, there was a moment of sheer athleticism that momentarily silenced the Kentucky throng and perhaps planted just the slightest doubt in previously certain minds. As five feet, six inch Willie Worsley approached the board for a standard layup, he did the seemingly impossible. He leaped into the air and dunked the ball. The intake of air was audible throughout the auditorium. It was as if Superman had leaped over a tall building. If the *little* guy on the Miner team could do that, what could the big guys do?

All this time, I was preparing my opponents for what they were about to face. I stared menacingly at the Kentucky players almost continuously. When it came my turn, I took the ball and dunked my customary dozen times, slamming the ball home with such force that the backstop rattled and shook as if it might splinter apart. Then I would glare back at the Kentucky team to make the point that ours was a team like no other the Rupp's Runts had faced. Tonight was ours.

Coach Haskins had no pre-game talk for us. I think he was out of words at that point. Across the court, the band was playing its tenth rendition of Dixie. Just before we took the court, Coach Haskins told Bobby Joe not to try to steal the ball. "They're too fast for that," he said. An unsuccessful steal attempt would leave the player with the ball uncovered and able to take an open shot. Bobby Joe grinned and looked at the coach. "How many times you want me to steal it?"

No one needed to tell me what to do. Coach Haskins and I had been on the same page all season. I don't recall him saying anything to me, but Haskins told Fitzpatrick that he told me, "I want you to take it to the guy [under the basket] and show him something he hasn't seen." Regardless, that was exactly what I had in mind.

On the Kentucky side, Adolph Rupp told his team to start the game man-to-man. Put pressure on them, he reportedly said. They'll self destruct sooner or later, or words to that effect.

As I reached the center of the court for the tip off, I leaned towards the Kentucky center, Thad Jaracz, and said something intimidating that only he could hear. He just looked at me with disbelief and didn't respond.

On Kentucky's first possession, they spread out into their trademark fastbreak. Riley took the ball and went in for a layup. You'll recall that it was our practice to make a point with the opposing team's star outright, even if we drew a foul doing it. I went up with Riley and slammed the ball, and Riley, to the floor, hard. I took the foul without complaint, figuring I had made my point.

With the free throw, Kentucky took a 1-0 lead. It would be the only time they led all night. We now got the ball, and it was passed to me under our basket. Their center, Jaracz, sort of vanished, though Riley came over to defend. I went up and slammed the ball hard through the basket with both hands. It was the kind of take-no-prisoners dunk I had mastered, and once down I stared into Riley's eyes. The white Kentucky crowd emitted a low "wooo," almost like a moan.

About that first dunk, Kron has said, "We were all kind of standing there and he soared up and it seemed to be a real exclamation point. It really picked their team up and I think we were intimidated to the extent that we didn't go to the boards as hard as we could. I kept going, but I was always late. They were already up there."

I'd scouted this team and knew what I could do. In those first two or three minutes, I abandoned the basket and went out to contest every shot, leaving my man wide open. It was up to my teammates to rebound. I'd seen Kentucky play and understood what they depended on. They would run and someone would be open, then he would make the jump shot.

But not tonight. Nothing was going uncontested. I was on the shooter, sometimes as a double team, sometimes alone, making my other statement. No one was going to be open. No one was getting a clear shot. This was going to be a game like no other they'd ever played.

Flournoy's knee was giving him a lot of trouble, and I was surprised that he even started. Not long into the game, he came out for good and Nevil Shed came in. We held Kentucky to 9 points in the first ten minutes, then Bobby Joe went in for a layup and was catapulted into the stands. No foul was called, and Bobby Joe walked back onto the court furious. Kentucky had made an enormous mistake. As they moved the ball down the court, Bobby Joe whipped around Dampier, stole the ball, and went in for an easy layup. Ten seconds later, he stole the ball from Dampier again and once more laid up the ball. They had made him mad with his brother watching, and they were going to pay the price. Whatever energy Kentucky had managed after those first ugly moments with my dunk vanished. They were shocked.

All season, no one had stolen the ball from them like that, twice in a row, and it seemed to take some of the starch out of a faltering team. "I wish I could forget those two steals," Dampier said years later. "I wish I could say that he fouled me, but he didn't. I was changing directions, dribbling with my left hand...and then it was gone. I can never forget it."

The steals were followed by another one of my dunks.

Seeing what appeared to be a mismatch, Kentucky wasted a lot of time trying to get Conley free. They seemed to think that because Worsley was eight inches shorter, he couldn't guard the man. They were wrong.

For the rest of the game, Kentucky tried to run, and we refused to let them. We had controlled the tempo of every game all season, and this one was no different. The attention and energy against the outside shooter threw off the Kentucky game. I owned the lower court, just as I expected, and no Kentucky player penetrated to good effect.

On defense, Kentucky played both man-to-man and its 1-3-1 zone, neither with much success. When they tried the zone, it tended to slow the game down, playing into our hands. This meant that only Kentucky's center, Jaracz, was on me, a player I could manhandle at will. It was murder down there.

Throughout the entire game, we played smart, the way we played all season. We surrendered no layups and gave up no turnovers. Our defense was designed to deny the pass for the fast break, to have someone on every player every time, and it worked that night as it had all season.

On the offense, our guards whipped the ball back and forth around the perimeter until one of the Kentucky players found himself out of position, and then they would take it in. At one point, Cager drove right through the vaunted Kentucky defense and dunked the ball with one hand.

As the Texas Western players ran down court, some of them made a point to run the lane closest to Adolph Rupp. They would give him a look, perhaps utter a word to try to catch his attention. Kentucky was experiencing a level of toughness and skill they had never seen before.

I dunked again, to the same demoralizing effect. As the little school from El Paso turned away every attempt at a comeback, Kentucky became increasingly desperate, fouling repeatedly, putting the Miners on the free throw line. Over one stretch, we hit 26 of 27 free throws.

At halftime, with his Miners in control of the game and leading, Coach Haskins had little to say, as had been the case for the second half of the regular season. He had done his part earlier on. They were winning. What was there to talk about? His primary concern was that we not let up, and he told us we should be winning by more.

In the Kentucky locker room, the situation could not have been more different. I depend on Fitzpatrick and others for this. Adolph Rupp, I've read, was ranting. His dreams of a fifth championship were vanishing before his eyes. Worse was who was beating his favorite team. "You aren't going to let those coons beat you, are you?" he screamed, according to several sources including noted sportswriter Frank Deford who was in the room. Deford also wrote that Rupp turned to Thad Jaracz and said, "You go after the big coon. You hear me?"

I was told that Jaracz leaned over and told his teammate, "If he thinks it's so easy why doesn't he go out there and get him himself?"

Conley said later that Texas Western "had the best defense we saw all year. They really came after you."

Deford reported that it seemed to him the Kentucky players turned their faces away in embarrassment at the racist words. Contrary to published reports, there were no racial slurs among the players, though the same could not be said of the Kentucky crowd, from what I've read. It was a businesslike effort for both teams, and I was so into the game that I heard nothing from the fans.

With Kentucky's losing effort, I made my final dunk. Jaracz said to me, "Nice play."

Kentucky pulled within one point twice during the second half, but Orsten and Bobby Joe repeatedly came up with key shots to stop them. Kentucky had no inside game. I saw to that. All they had were challenged jump shots, and as the game wound down, they began to foul us, hoping we would lose the game at the free throw line. We converted 28 of 34. I didn't miss one.

The referees called the game straight, though Kentucky fans complained about the disparity. They had 23 to our 12, but that was because they were intentionally fouling or fouling out of desperation towards the end. With about seven minutes to go in the game, Orsten made a jumper, then Bobby Joe stole the ball again, and I followed up with a dunk. We were ahead 60-51. Not much later, trying to steal the ball from Worsley, Conley fouled out of the game.

One of the unfortunate consequences of the game was that subsequent news accounts portrayed the Kentucky players as racists, as if the game could not have had the significance it held without words being spoken, as if all-white and all-black wasn't enough. I was there. It didn't happen. The Kentucky team was, and remains, a group of guys with class.

As the game wound down, some noticed that Coach Haskins had not yet sent in one of his four white bench players. The game was being played with the seven black players, or six since Flournoy never came back in. Later Coach Haskins said he had played his best players; isn't that what a coach is supposed to do if he wants to win?

Over the years, Coach Haskins has stuck with that version of events. If it's true, then why didn't Jerry Armstrong play?

He'd had a great game the night before, he was a senior, the only senior not to play. But Jerry was white.

I've always seen it another way. Coach Haskins had, in effect, been dared to try to beat Kentucky with black players. As the clock ran down and the victory became more and more certain, he elected to stay with his African-American starters. Jerry was deeply disappointed at not getting to play at least a few minutes, but years later he saw it very differently, "I guess the game was bigger than life itself," he said.

> WHEN THAT CLOCK STARTED TICKING OFF, IT SEEMED LIKE THE WHOLE WORLD JUST STOOD STILL.

I think Coach Haskins was making a point. He intended to beat Adolph Rupp with an all-black team. Over the years, time and again, I've read about how we won with five black starters. True enough, but the greater truth is we beat an all-white team with all-black players. Coach Haskins wanted no room for interpretation but the obvious one.

The final moments were anti-climatic, with the Texas Western guards moving into keep-away, passing the ball back and forth as we ran out the clock. "Oh, how I can remember those last seven seconds," Nevil Shed said later. "When that clock started ticking off, it seemed like the whole world just stood still.... Five, four, three.... We were going to beat Kentucky. We were going to win the national championship."

For me, I was in my game, in my rhythm. I never wanted to stop playing. We owned this team and no matter what they tried, they weren't going to beat us. Riley later said that if we had played three times, Texas Western would have beaten Kentucky three times.

When the final buzzer sounded, the arena broke into a great quiet. The celebration was limited to the Texas Western bench and all 250 of our fans, many of whom ran onto the court. I think if you find a tape of that moment in the game, you'll see everybody there who was rooting for us in a single camera shot.

The once-frenzied Kentucky crowd sat in stunned silence. And I mean silence. Their band wasn't playing Dixie. No one brandished a Confederate battle flag. There was no taunting by whites against us. Any claim of white supremacy in basketball that night was settled, though probably not to their way of thinking.

The white sportswriters didn't know what to make of the upset. At first the story line was that this little school in West Texas upset the Kentucky powerhouse; they were incapable of dealing with what had really happened. I read *Sports Illustrated's* article, and there's not a single word about race. And no one, no one white at least, initially grasped what had just been accomplished, what racial myths had been slain, what lies could no longer be told or believed. What I'm saying is that the major news stories never mentioned that an all-black team had defeated an all-white team.

Coach Iba reached over and enthusiastically shook Coach Haskins's hand. For the first time in a long time, Coach Haskins smiled. The relief must have been enormous. He said later he felt not so much elation as he did relief that the difficult season was over.

Across the court, it appeared that tears were going down Riley's face, while Conley couldn't bear to watch the presentation ceremony coming up. "We never had a game like that [before]," Kron said.

When it was over, I didn't want to take any of the glory, though I was certain that, had I gone to the basket, the others would have stood aside. Given my role, I knew I could have cut the net down, grabbed the trophy, held it high overhead in triumph. I believe my teammates would have seen it as my due. Had Bobby Joe done the same thing, they might have seen it that way for him.

As it was, Willie Worsley climbed on Willie Cager's shoulders and cut the nets down, from both ends. Coach Haskins had the three seniors on our team—Orsten Artis, Harry Flournoy and Jerry Armstrong—accept the NCAA trophy on behalf of us and Texas Western.

I found myself in the role of a spectator, and I stood aside watching the others with great jubilation. We had played so well—I had played so well—I wanted the game to go on and on. We had played all season for this, and I wanted to enjoy it more. There was time for celebrating later. But I liked how it felt to win it all, how good I felt, and part of me couldn't wait to get back the next year.

We won 72 to 65 in a game that was even less of a contest than the final score suggests. The statistics told the story. Kentucky made 27 of 70 attempts at field goals for 38.5% while we connected on 22 of 49 for 44.9% and shot with deadly accuracy from the free throw line, sinking 28 of 34 to Kentucky's 11 of 13.

I scored 16 points, second only to Bobby Joe's 20, this despite the fact that I sat out for 11 minutes. I pulled down nine rebounds and blocked six shots, this against not only the number one basketball team in the country, but also the best team Adolph Rupp ever had. I also shot six of six from the free throw line and was five for ten in field goals.

I was absolutely convinced that my decision to contest every shot had been pivotal. Our defense the entire game had been outstanding, the best we had played all season, but even in man-to-man, an opponent will get free once in awhile. In most cases when this happened, I was right there. The result was that Kentucky rarely had an uncontested shot.

Frank Deford, writing for *Sports Illustrated,* said the game had been "a lost cause almost from the start," so overwhelming was our play. It had turned out to be the Kentucky offense against our defense, the way games usually went according to the game plan Coach Haskins designed, and our defense had won. Abe Lemons, the Oklahoma City University coach, said, "They [Texas Western] didn't get a single break against Kentucky that I saw, yet they broke 'em right down and were in the saddle all the way."

To win the NCAA national championship we had defeated four conference champions. These were Cincinnati of the Missouri Valley, Kansas of the Big Eight, Utah of the Western Athletic, and Kentucky of the Southeastern. It was a monumental achievement, especially by a college no one had ever heard of.

The white media were in such a state of shock, no one interviewed the Miner players until years later. The Kentucky team did not come to us on the court and congratulate us as is customary. Adolph Rupp refused to enter the locker room and congratulate Coach Haskins. Pat Riley and Louie Dampier were the only Kentucky players to come to the Texas Western locker room and congratulate us, I'm told, though I didn't see them, and they didn't congratulate me.

Pat Riley sensed that something remarkable had happened. Years later he said, "We had no idea what we were getting into. In those days, players didn't dunk. I hadn't seen anyone dunk. Guys barely jumped high enough to stick a dollar bill under their shoes. But these guys came out, and after they dunked on me about three times, I knew they had a lot more to accomplish than we did."

Years later, I asked Coach Haskins which of the Kentucky players he would have started on our team if he'd had that choice. He thought a long time and finally said, "None. None of them would have been a starter." Kentucky was a very, very good team. You don't lose just one game, advance to the national championship game, and not be very good, but we weren't just better as a team; each of our players in his position was superior to his Kentucky counterpart.

On our team, it fell to Bobby Joe to first comprehend what had happened. As Fitzpatrick relates the story, Bobby Joe's older brother told him at the team party that the Texas Western victory had been historic.

"What do you mean?" Bobby Joe asked.

"It's the first time five blacks have beaten five whites in a game like this."

Bobby Joe thought for a moment then said, "Wow." Until that moment he hadn't thought about it that way. None of us had.

CHAPTER 12

STUNNED

It was a violent game. I don't mean there were any fights, but they were desperate and they were committed and they were more motivated than we were.

KENTUCKY'S PAT RILEY

OF ALL THE PLAYERS on our team, I have to say that Nevil Shed, Willie Worsley, and Willie Cager were the most visibly excited about winning. They were from New York City, and one of the biggest programs on television at the time was Sunday night's *Ed Sullivan Show* broadcast from Manhattan. It was the custom for the winning NCAA team to make an appearance on the program, and they were just thrilled at the prospect.

But we received no invitation, and we didn't appear, the only NCAA basketball championship team of the era not to be invited. If that doesn't say something to you about the times, it should.

The night of the game, Adolph Rupp wasn't prepared to meet with reporters until after midnight. Earlier that very day, he had said that his Runts would be the best team he'd ever coached—if they won. I think when he said that, he fully expected that his team would handle us easily. I've read that he was never one to accept the slightest responsibility for a loss, so this night was no different. "The pressure got to us. Riley was as tight as a drum. Jaracz didn't play much of a game. Kron wasn't feeling well and he gave out. We didn't shoot well and we didn't handle the ball well either."

Asked what he thought of the play of Bobby Joe Hill, Rupp was quoted saying, "Ah, he was a good little boy. But everybody's got a good little boy."

Rupp's response to the loss has been described as "ungracious." One reporter said that he "went to his grave never forgiving" us for the defeat. Fitzpatrick quotes a long-time unnamed Rupp acquaintance, "Don't let anyone tell you any different. Adolph hated each and every loss in his career. But that one hit him like a ton of bricks. And the reason ought to be obvious. The man was under pressure for not recruiting blacks, he was being criticized for that even by people at his own school. Then he goes and loses an NCAA championship game to an all-black team. Think of how humiliating that was for him. He was repudiated. That's why it stung the man."

Pat Riley is quoted as saying that Adolph Rupp left the arena clutching a bottle of Bourbon. The Kentucky players returned to their hotel for iced beer in their rooms. They were dog tired. One described the events after the loss as an out-of-body experience. Fitzpatrick quotes Kron saying, "We did try. We just came up short and got beat by a good team. It wasn't a fluke. Everybody always said if we played them ten times, we would win nine. If I've heard that once, I've heard it a thousand times. It's Kentucky people trying to justify what happened. Kentucky people have a tough time losing. Well, it's never going to happen again. We played them once and we got beat."

Arriving back in Lexington, there was an obligation on the part of the Kentucky players and coach to address those 5,000 die-hard fans who turned out to greet them. I'm sure it wasn't easy. Conley even apologized. "I'm sorry," he said. "We did the best we could."

When Adolph Rupp spoke he said, "It was regrettable that we got so far and were not up for the game. Our shots just would not drop. The boys provided us with a wonderful winter of entertainment. I don't believe any team in history received as much publicity as they did."

There was no hesitation in El Paso about what this meant. We were number one. Everybody who lived in El Paso, it seemed, greeted us at the airport or lined the route through town to the campus. Baudoin told a reporter, "Afterwards, we were half happy and half amazed. We wanted to get out of Maryland very badly and get back home. When we did, it was like Mars. There was an ocean of people all the way from the airport to the campus."

We just couldn't believe the outpouring of emotion. The college had never been in the final NCAA game before, never even reached the Final Four. Now they were national champions. Texas Western was the first, and so far only, Texas team to win the NCAA tournament. I remain the only native Texan ever to start the winning team of the NCAA tournament.

In sleepy El Paso, fans poured into the streets the moment the victory was official, though by then it was well after midnight. They jubilantly gathered on the Texas Western campus or at San Jacinto Plaza in the center of town. For some reason, fire hydrants were even opened. A vast convoy of cars drove round and round, drivers and passengers shouting, honking horns. Everywhere the endless pealing of the church bells could be heard.

At one intersection, a bonfire was started that grew in size and intensity as wood was thrown into the flames. Finally, students tore down tree limbs to add to the inferno, then tossed in their caps and shirts. The blaze grew so enormous that the fire department was summoned to be certain it didn't spread. One firefighter was injured by a falling branch and was taken to the hospital. The street party lasted through the night and then was carried out to the airport as we arrived shortly after eight o'clock in the morning.

The waiting crowd that had come to the little airport from the college campus and downtown to greet us was so vast that the pilot took a pass over the field for us to see it before landing. I've read one report that said the pilot *had* to make the pass because the crowd was standing on the runway. Nevil Shed described the scene from the air as "fantastic." Once the airplane came to a stop, Willie Cager exitedly brandished the trophy for the screaming fans to see.

We were all taken to a stand for a brief ceremony where local dignitaries spoke. There was the college band and another from the town made up of Mariachis. The police appeared to be as excited as the crowd. What a great day. The crowd asked for Bobby Joe, and Coach Haskins explained he had flown home to be with his dying father. He then continued speaking, but not for long. "To tell you the truth, I can't yet believe it's reality. The fans and community provided us with tremendous support during the season."

FOR THE FIRST TIME BEGAN TO CONSIDER THAT WE HAD ACCOMPLISHED EVEN MORE THAN WE THOUGHT.

Worn out, he had the chief of police drive him straight home from the airport and skipped the rest of the festivities. The team rode to the campus in a parade, greeted along the way by a crowd estimated at 10,000, the biggest ever seen up to that time in El Paso. That day and thereafter, for the rest of the year, we were heros. In fact, I cannot to this day walk the streets of the town without being thanked and congratulated on the victory.

A few days after the game, Coach Haskins gathered us and read a telegram from comedian Bill Cosby, telling us what the victory had meant to him and other black Americans, how it had changed how he felt. I was deeply moved and for the first time began to consider that we had accomplished even more than we thought.

At Kentucky's season-ending banquet in Lexington, the master of ceremonies was the sports editor for the Lexington *Herald-Leader*. At one point he remarked, "At least we're still the number one white team in the country." Present were black high school athletes that the college president hoped to recruit as well as black high school coaches. They wanted to see for themselves that his program was not racist. The editor was fired.

If the reporters that night in the arena and in the weeks to follow didn't know what to make of what they had just witnessed, African-Americans across the nation had watched and knew. They understood and were energized. No one had stared that night at the television of white America and said, "Look, Mom. There's one of us."

It was another advance in the Civil Rights Movement and a turning point in collegiate sports. Young black men playing ball suddenly had new opportunities. NFL great Chuck Foreman watched the game and said years later, "All of us who were young [athletes] saw that '66 game and felt like there was hope for us. [It] gave black people a chance."

Much later, one newspaper called the game "a fairy tale," all the more significant because it had been played against the backdrop of the struggle of the nation's Civil Rights Movement.

White Americans also saw the game, and, for many, stereotypes fell away. If the myth about black players was false, what other beliefs about blacks were also untrue? Because the insight was so new and unexpected, the shock of the game lingered, and it was some time before the full impact settled in.

From what I've read, Adolph Rupp continued giving Texas Western no respect. "… They just whipped us. That's the story of the game," he said. Explaining why Kentucky had no black basketball players, Rupp said, "So far we haven't found a boy who meets our scholastic qualifications. It's got to be a Kentucky boy or from a neighbor state. We can't go raid some schoolyard.... I hate to see those boys from Texas Western win it. Not because of race or anything like that, but because of the type of recruiting it represents...don't you think I could put together a championship team, if I went out and got every kid who could jam a ball through a hoop?"

Yes, indeed. Those dunks had really hurt.

I guess he wasn't alone. Defeat can be difficult to accept. Kentucky president John W. Oswald said, "I think what happened to that Texas Western team was really pretty outrageous. None of those players, as I understand, ever went on for another semester, much less graduated." Nothing could have been further from the truth. What unfortunate lies.

In 1975, Adolph Rupp was interviewed for the local newspaper and said that his "all-time favorite team" had lost the 1966 NCAA final to a "bunch of crooks." He claimed that the biggest upset of his career was "not winning in '66 and finding out Texas Western had all those ineligible players...one was on parole from Tennessee State Prison (me). Two had been kicked out of a junior college in Iowa. Texas Western was suspended by the NCAA for three years after that."

Let's set the record straight. I was never in Tennessee State Prison, on parole from it or anywhere else. I went to college in Tennessee, period. And no one on the team was "kicked out" of any junior college. Texas Western was *not* suspended for anything, let alone recruiting violations, not then or ever. There were no recruiting violations. Yes, the recruitment of that fine team was in some ways unorthodox, but it was entirely proper and aboveboard. The great tragedy of that game is that those lies persist to this day.

Despite the lies, all-white teams across America fell like so many dominoes. The SEC began integrating immediately. Barely a month after the game, all-white Vanderbilt signed its first black player. Kentucky was never in the championship game again until it had black players. The tide had turned. No longer did talented high school players disappear into obscurity because they had nowhere to go.

The percentage of black collegiate basketball players went from 10 percent in 1966 to 34 percent in a few short years. In 1974, the once all-white University of Alabama started five black players. In 1991, 19 of the 20 starters on the four top-seeded teams for the NCAA tournament were African-American. The change we brought was a strong shift and total.

With some time for reflection, the national media behaved as if Texas Western had stolen the championship. There was little mention of race in the immediate news coverage. You won't see it in the *Sports Illustrated* article or in the one that ran in *The New York Times*. I've read that that was because it was feared there would be rioting if the obvious was reported and there was a general desire not to acknowledge the social significance of what had happened.

There were, inevitable, nasty columns by white columnists, generally smearing the character of our players. One attacked the Texas Western academics, not mentioning that of the five players Kentucky recruited the previous year, four flunked out of school.

In 1968, Jack Olsen published an infamous series in *Sports Illustrated* titled *Black Athletes: A Shameful Story*. The title says it all, and Olsen devoted some attention to Texas Western. He wrote of the difficulties experienced by young black athletes recruited by predominantly white colleges to play sports. No one said change would be easy, and rather than point to the positives, Olsen elected to write about the negatives. I won't repeat any of it, but the story has lingered in the decades since as if everything it said was an accurate representation of how things stood.

One of the ugliest, and most unfortunate, attacks on the victory was by best-selling novelist, James A. Michener. Ten years after the event, he gave three pages to the game in his book, *Sports in America,* and wrote that "The El Paso story is one of the most wretched in the history of American sports. I have often thought how much luckier the white players were under Coach Adolph Rupp. He looked after his players; they had a shot at a real education; and they were secure within the traditions of their university, their community and their state."

About our performance during the game Michener wrote, "The Texas Western blacks straggled on [the court], a bunch of loose-jointed ragamuffins ready for a brawl." He described us as "five tough New York playground types" who were "conscripted" to play. We were "hopelessly outclassed...furious young men who had come to wrestle the ball away, flood the forecourt with shooters, and keep throwing the basketball toward the basket until it went in."

Michener also repeated the false claim, as did many others, that none of those on our team graduated from college and called us "poorly paid gladiators" who were "tossed aside when their eligibility was exhausted."

Such comments, those of Adolph Rupp, and those of other sportswriters have survived many years later, blatant lies though they be. This is all so offensive and untrue that it is incredibly disappointing to have to respond to it at all. Michener's outrageous lies are still in his book, never corrected, and young scholars preparing reports consult it, thinking the great novelist actually knew what he was talking about.

The players from Texas Western aren't the only ones to be deeply offended by these lies, which St. Louis sports historian Chuck Korr has said were the result of efforts by Adolph Rupp and others to divert blame for the loss. "Rupp was to basketball like Michener was to literature; if he said it, it was going to stick. People had to find some way to diminish [Texas Western's] accomplishment."

Willie Worsley observed, "There were some people on the team…a little angry at being forgotten, because at that time when teams would win the national championship, you would see them on TV all the time. We never got on TV. They still treated us like second-class citizens. The town treated us like King Tut, but no one else. And there were some black militants and people on both sides that wanted to make a big deal out of things [written about us]."

At home, Coach Haskins faced a firestorm of hatred, receiving an estimated 40,000 pieces of hate mail from all across the nation. Again and again he was told that it was not good to have so many black players on his team. He was roundly criticized for exploiting black athletes to advance his own career. "We filled up trash baskets with those letters," Haskins said. "People from all over were calling my players names that started with the little letter 'n'. White people were saying I used them to win games. Black people said I had exploited the players…."

Willie Worsley said it best for all of us: "I would never have gone to college without an athletic scholarship. Who used who?"

Though we elected not to speak of it at the time, many of the players received threatening telephone calls and letters. Bobby Joe had his life threatened. I changed my telephone number three times, but the calls kept coming.

Back in Houston that summer, I was greeted as a conquering hero everywhere I went, but in the black community the impact was even greater. While I had been focused on winning a game, on proving we were the best, they talked about what the victory meant and expressed joy, elation, and profound emotion. It would be more than a decade before I came to understand what the game represented. It took America at least that long.

I like to think that the impact, of my dunks in that game, was not lost on white coaches across America. My in-your-face, intimidating style of play had been showcased on a national stage. Many watching the game didn't know such a move was possible and were seeing it for the first time. My slam dunks, along with Cager's, were largely credited for the victory. Several people also mentioned Bobby Joe's awesome steals.

Lew Alcindor (later, Kareem Abdul-Jabbar) and Elvin Hayes were to launch their varsity play the next year. Adolph Rupp and others lobbied and persuaded the NCAA to outlaw the dunk for ten long years in a futile attempt to "save" basketball from black players.

I have no doubt who Adolph Rupp was thinking about when he demanded the rule change.

CHAPTER 13

MAKING HISTORY

We may never have gotten our just due....

People say your reward is in heaven.

Our reward will be in history.

TEXAS WESTERN'S WILLIE WORSLEY

OVER THE YEARS, THERE has been a slow realization among us that we have been part of something that was good, something that brought about lasting change.

If that awareness was slow in coming, at least I had understood from the first what it would have meant if we had been beaten by Kentucky. That moment of revelation standing on the sidelines, watching Kentucky warm up, had told me. They would have said, "We told you so. Black players can't win at that level." It might have been years before another predominantly black team with all-black starters was in the position we had been in. The point would have been made. The men in hoods, riding in the backs of pickup trucks with shotguns, would have been energized. The very thought was sobering.

Entering the 1966 NCAA basketball season, all-white, or white-dominated, teams had won every previous national championship. We changed that for good. Sportswriter David Israel called the game the "Brown v. Board of Education of college basketball." Basketball historian Neil D. Isaacs wrote,

"Since that time, no pretender to basketball eminence has ever drawn a color line in its recruiting."

The Kentucky players have been unjustly portrayed, as well. Tommy Kron said years later, "The only thing that bothers me is that some people think we were motivated by that, by playing an all-black team. That was certainly not the case at all. To me, that's ignorance, and we didn't deserve that. All we cared about was winning the game."

Pat Riley, NBA all-star, MVP and storied coach, for one, has tried to set the record straight for his fellow white Kentucky players. He told *Sports Illustrated* he considered the game "the ultimate" in sportsmanship and was proud to have been part of what he lightly called "the Emancipation Proclamation of 1966."

"It was one of the most significant games ever played because it dispelled the absurd illusions that too many people in this country held to be true. It was one of the worst nights of my life...but I'm still proud to be part of something that changed the lives of so many people," said Pat Riley in 1996.

On another occasion, Riley said it this way: "When he came to the Lakers, Bob McAdoo told me how much the game meant, how it changed everything, how it opened up the world for black kids in the South. I guess I never really thought of it that way, that we were such a big part of history. The loss remains. I've never felt emptier. It was the worst night of my basketball life, but I'm proud to have taken part in something that changed so many other people's lives."

Larry Conley said in 1999, "I don't know that people see us as bad guys. I think they see the game as representation of change. I've talked to a lot of African-American leaders, politicians, coaches of a certain age, and they saw the game as part of social change, a turning point. The Voting Rights Act passed in 1964. It was a turbulent time, there was a lot going on. Let's face it, there were a lot of things in society then that needed to change. I think people see that game as part of the change."

Bobby Joe later said, "To us, it was just a game. Just go play. To everybody else, it was black versus white, that undertone. And, right, the game did change a lot of things. I mean, it was five blacks against five whites on national television for the whole money. And it was in the 1960's."

> THAT'S WHAT
> A COACH IS
> SUPPOSED TO DO,
> GIVE YOUR TEAM
> ITS BEST CHANCE.

Turning points aren't always seen for what they mean at the time, and this one was obscured by negative commentary. The myth that we destroyed, was that black people couldn't think, didn't have the ability to do anything of significance. American sports and culture were never again the same after our trailblazing win. By the twentieth anniversary of the victory, I had come to understand that this was our legacy to collegiate basketball.

In 1986, El Paso held a reunion for us, and we were all able to attend. It was wonderful to see everyone again. When we had won the national championship we were given watches. Now a local businessman paid for rings, and we were each presented with one, which is now my most prized possession.

Coach Haskins stood by what he said at the time. "I just played the five best players, that's all. That's what a coach is supposed to do, isn't it, give your team its best chance?"

"This may never happen to me again," Haskins had said, and it never did. He never returned to the Final Four in a career with 719 wins and 353 losses. The tragedy of his success is that the lies told have taken on a life of their own. If fairly treated, his program should have had greater success than it did.

Adolph Rupp never won another NCAA title.

It's my book so here is my record: I averaged 19.3 points a game in NCAA play, along with 10.6 rebounds. I remain the all-time Texas Western (UTEP) scoring leader, this even though I only played two years varsity ball. In my final college game I scored 34 points, my best, with 13 rebounds. Just six feet, seven inches tall, I dominated the center, often against much larger players. I scored in double figures in 44 of 56 college games. I had double figure rebounds in 27 games. I was named the MVP in the Midwest Regional with 44 points and 25 rebounds against Cincinnati and Kansas.

I only played another season for Texas Western, which was named that year the University of Texas at El Paso, or UTEP. Though we had a good season, we were hampered by injuries to Bobby Joe, who decided to drop out of college to support his family. That's the only reason he wasn't an All-American again that year, as I was. By the end of the year, my mother had become ill, and I made the decision to play professional basketball. I was the number one pick by the NBA San Francisco Warriors in 1967, the seventh pick overall in the draft. Playing in the NBA allowed me to become good friends with my idol Wilt Chamberlain. I also got to play with Nat Thurmon at Golden State.

The next year, I spent a season with the Phoenix Suns, then in 1969, began my play with the Harlem Globetrotters. In 1970, I signed with the American Basketball Association Pittsburgh Condors and played with them two seasons, then went to the Memphis Tams of the ABA, before returning to the Harlem Globetrotters in 1973 for three years.

In both the NBA and ABA, I missed playing with the Texas Western team. I missed the camaraderie, the cohesiveness, the self-sacrifice. I just didn't experience it at the next level. I did come away, however, with the firm belief that, if the NCAA championship team had a seven foot center, it would be good enough to win it all in the NBA. Coach Haskins was certainly good enough to have won at that level as well.

My years with the Globetrotters were the most enjoyable of my career. I played with Meadowlark Lemon and Curly Neal. This was a great experience, because for once I was trying to make people happy, to see smiling faces in the crowd. It was because of my play with the Globetrotters that I met the president face to face.

Though Coach Haskins had, from time to time, regretted the turmoil that surrounded that win, I personally never have. I'd prepared myself all my life to be on the public stage, and playing on the team that won the NCAA basketball championship put me there. All that work, for all those years, had been to that end.

So many lies have been told about us, for so many years, please allow me to set the record straight. We all went on to live fine lives:

Bobby Joe Hill worked as a buyer for the El Paso Natural Gas company until his untimely death from a heart attack at the age of 59.

Harry Flournoy graduated from Texas Western and works in management for Orowheat.

Willie Worsley graduated from Texas Western and works as the director of a children's academy in New York City.

Nevil Shed graduated from Texas Western and works at a university in San Antonio.

Willie Cager graduated from Texas Western and is head basketball coach at a high school in El Paso.

Orsten Artis graduated from Texas Western and retired as a detective in Gary, Indiana.

So there is no doubt here, let me do some repeating. Nine of the 12 players on that championship team graduated from college. Nine out of 12.

It may surprise some that Bobby Joe didn't stick out that last season in college, even after being known for helping win the championship. I believe he could have had a fantastic NBA career. If he had, I think he would be a household name, but the NBA didn't pay all that well at the time. For the 1968-69 season, for example, the NBA increased the minimum rookie salary to $10,000. That's right, $10,000. Bobby Joe would have made a decent living as a pro player, and he'd have been paid more than the minimum, but his decision not to pursue a professional career isn't as strange as it might first appear. The years of the big salaries for professional players were still down the road, something I learned in my NBA and ABA play.

I've read that Adolph Rupp mellowed in his later years. In 1977, the year he died, he spoke at the Final Four tournament in Atlanta. He talked about college basketball as "this wonderful tapestry that brought people together from different creeds and colors...." Maybe he believed it. I hope he did.

Adolph Rupp was forced into retirement at the age of 70 with a total 876 wins and his four national championships. "I still wake up in the middle of the night wondering what I could have done differently to help my boys win that game," he's been quoted as saying. His biographer wrote that he carried the memory of that one defeat to the end of his days.

Over the years, I've come to believe that, if we had beaten Utah or all-white Duke in that final game, it wouldn't have become so significant. The game has come to mean so much, not because we beat an all-white team, though I don't think that would have gone unnoticed, but because we beat Adolph Rupp. I think Harry Flournoy said it just right, "No one will remember him without remembering us. And I guess there is a certain justice to that."

At our twentieth anniversary gathering, Coach Haskins said, "You guys got a lot of black kids scholarships around this country. You can be proud of that. I guess you helped change the world a little bit."

Talking to young blacks today, I find that it's very difficult for them to understand the world in which I was raised: segregated schools, black and white drinking fountains. Bill Russell talked about cross burning in his neighborhood when he was playing for a winning Celtics team. Some didn't want a black man in their neighborhood, no matter what.

Prejudice is still there. You don't see it as much, and it isn't just white people against black; there are blacks prejudiced against white people. Some people just don't like others because of their color. I've wondered from time to time; if we were all the same color, whom would these people hate? Racism is simply in the nature of the society in which we live, and we all learn to deal with it as best we can.

The great lesson of that 1966 NCAA college championship game isn't about white or black. It's that we are all God's children, every one of us.

My mother passed some years ago, but her wisdom has remained, so let me close with what she taught me: We can't allow ourselves to hate others because others hate us. She believed that and lived it. That's what I believe and have tried to live. I think that game helped others to follow what Mom taught.

●

Pursue the course set before you,

watch keenly for opportunities,

do what you know to do and God

will see that you are in the right place at the

right time to cross paths with your destiny.

ANDREA GARNEY

Bracket

UNIV. OF HOUSTON (82)		
Wichita, Kansas 3-7-66		**HOUSTON**
COLORADO STATE (76)		Los Angeles 3-11-66
	BYE	**OREGON STATE**
	BYE	**COLLEGE OF PACIFIC**
	BYE	Los Angeles 3-11-66
		UTAH
TEXAS WESTERN COLLEGE (89)		
Wichita, Kansas 3-7-66		**TWC (78)**
OKLAHOMA CITY COLLEGE (77)		Lubbock 3-11-66
	BYE	**CINCINNATI (76)**
	BYE	
	BYE	**SMU**
		Lubbock 3-11-66
WESTERN KENTUCKY		**KANSAS**
Kent, Ohio		
CHICAGO LOYOLA		**WESTERN KENTUCKY**
	BYE	Iowa City 3-11-66
		MICHIGAN
DAYTON		
Kent, Ohio		**DAYTON**
MIAMI OF OHIO		Iowas City 3-11-66
	BYE	**KENTUCKY**
ST. JOSEPHS PA		
Blacksburg, VA		**ST. JOSEPHS**
PROVIDENCE		Raleigh, NC 3-11-66
	BYE	**DUKE**
DAVIDSON		
Blaksburg, VA		**DAVIDSON**
RHODE ISLAND		Raleigh, NC 3-11-66
	BYE	**SYRACUSE**

KENTUCKY WILDCATS

PLAYER	FG	FT	Reb	PF	TP	Ast	FW	MP
Louis Dampier	7-18	5-5	9	4	19	1	6	40
Tommy Kron	3-6	0-0	7	2	6	3	5	33
Larry Conley	4-9	2-2	8	5	10	1	0	35
Pat Riley	8-22	3-4	4	4	19	1	2	20
Thad Jaracz	3-8	1-2	5	5	7	0	2	28
Cliff Berger	2-3	0-0	0	0	4	0	0	12
Gary Gamble	0-0	0-0	0	1	0	0	0	2
Jim LeMaster	0-1	0-0	0	1	0	0	0	3
Bob Tallent	0-3	0-0	0	1	0	0	1	7
TOTALS	27-70	11-13	33	23	65	6	16	200

Team Rebounds (Not Included in Above Totals)

1966 NCAA Basketball

OREGON STATE

Far West Regionals
Los Angeles 3-12-66

UTAH

UTAH (78)

Semi Finals
University of Maryland
3-18-66

TWC (85)

TWC (81)

Mid West Regionals
Lubbock 3-12-66

KANSAS (80)

TWC (72)

CHAMPIONSHIP GAME
COLE FIELD HOUSE
University of Maryland
March 19, 1966

TWC

MICHIGAN

Mid East Regionals
Iowa City 3-12-66

KENTUCKY

KENTUCKY (83)

Semi Finals
University of Maryland
3-18-66

KENTUCKY (65)

DUKE

Eastern Regionals
Raleigh, NC 3-12-66

SYRACUSE

DUKE (79)

TEXAS WESTERN MINERS

PLAYER	FG	FT	Reb	PF	TP	Ast	FW	MP
Bobby Joe Hill	7-17	6-9	3	3	20	3	6	40
Orsten Artis	5-13	5-5	8	1	15	0	1	40
Nevil Shed	1-1	1-1	3	1	3	0	2	12
David Lattin	5-10	6-6	9	4	16	0	0	32
Willie Cager	1-3	6-7	6	3	8	0	3	30
Harry Flournoy	1-1	0-4	5	0	2	0	0	6
Willie Worsley	2-4	4-16	7	0	8	1	6	40
TOTALS	22-49	28-34	35	12	72	4	18	200

Team Rebounds (Not Included in Above Totals)

Team Shooting Percentage		1st			2nd			3rd
	M	A	Pct.	M	A	Pct.	M	A	Pct.
Kentucky	23	35	65.7	14	35	40	27	70	38.5
Texas Western	12	29	41	10	22	45	22	49	44.8

ABOUT THE AUTHOR

DAVID L. LATTIN, an only child to his widowed mother Elsie, was born in Houston, Texas on December 23, 1943. Attending elementary and secondary schools in Houston, he graduated from Evan E. Worthing Senior High School in 1963.

Worthing High School, a new Houston high school in the early 60's, won the Texas 3-AAAA State Title in David's junior year. David was named all-state and All-American on several All-America high school teams, the first Texas schoolboy player, white or black, to ever be named to a high school All-America team. David was even better the following year, and again selected as an All-State (unanimous selection), an All-American player, and named the Most Valuable Player of the game.

David had a number of scholarship offers his senior year, which began a journey that led him to accept a full scholarship to Texas Western College to play for Coach Don Haskins and the rest is well-recorded history.

While at Texas Western (1965-1967), David led the Texas Western College team to the 1966 Division 1 NCAA National Championship, the only Texan to ever lead his high school team to a state basketball championship and his college team to the Division One Collegiate NCAA National Championship—a moment that changed history forever.

To this day, David still holds a number of school NCAA tournament records. He was named, at Texas Western, MVP of the Midwest Regional (NCAA) and All-American during both the 1966 and 1967 seasons.

While at Texas Western College, David, who majored in Radio & Television, also found time to host his own campus radio jazz and blues music show.

David's considerable size and talent as a gifted big man did not go unnoticed by the professional leagues and he was drafted number one by the San Francisco Warriors in 1967. David had a successful professional basketball career over a period of eight years, playing for the San Francisco Warriors, the Phoenix Suns, the Pittsburgh Condors, and the Memphis Tams, the latter two of the fledgling American Basketball Association (ABA), and the world famous Harlem Globetrotters.

Later, after his professional basketball career ended, David went on to complete his Bachelor of Science degree in Business Administration which laid the foundation for a successful business career. David has a diverse business portfolio as a real estate investor, as well as, affliations with beverage distribution companies, and he is also the President and CEO of Your Maison Housing.

David is the father of one son, Clifton, a daughter, Leslie, and he is the proud grandfather to eight grandchildren.

For additional information on seminars or scheduling speaking engagements, please send your correspondence to:

8633 West Airport, #125
Houston, Texas 77071

Or

UTEP43@aol.com

Please visit: www.lattinsdunk.com

Additional copies of this book are available
from your local bookstore.

If this book has touched your life,
we would like to hear from you.
Write us at:
info@whitestonebooks.com

WHITE STONE BOOKS
LAKELAND, FLORIDA